Quarterly Essay

CONTENTS

Quarterly Essay is published four times a year by Black Inc., an imprint of Schwartz Media Pty Ltd. Publisher: Morry Schwartz.

ISBN 978-1-86395-431-0 ISSN 1832-0953

Subscriptions – 1 year (4 issues): $49 within Australia incl. GST. Outside Australia $79.
2 years (8 issues): $95 within Australia incl. GST. Outside Australia $155.
Payment may be made by Mastercard, Visa or Bankcard, or by cheque made out to Schwartz Media. Payment includes postage and handling.

To subscribe, fill out and post the subscription card, or subscribe online at:

www.quarterlyessay.com

Correspondence and subscriptions should be addressed to the Editor at:

Black Inc. Level 5, 289 Flinders Lane Melbourne VIC 3000 Australia
Phone: 61 3 9654 2000 / Fax: 61 3 9654 2290
Email:
quarterlyessay@blackincbooks.com (editorial)
subscribe@blackincbooks.com (subscriptions)

Editor: Chris Feik / Management: Sophy Williams, Caitlin Yates. Publicity: Elisabeth Young / Design: Guy Mirabella. Production Co-ordinator: Adam Shaw

Printed in Australia by McPherson's Printing Group.

| STOP AT NOTHING | The Life and Adventures of Malcolm Turnbull |

Annabel Crabb

Malcolm Turnbull is standing in the business aisle of a Qantas flight, fiddling with his BlackBerry. We've just touched down in Sydney and are halfway through a discussion about military butlers, or "batmen," on which topic his assistant Nick Berry – a former army man – has offered certain insights. Within seconds of the seatbelt light blinking off, Turnbull is out of his seat and Googling. He is trying to look up the etymology of the word "batman," but his gadget won't work fast enough for him to find the answer before the queue of passengers behind him – polite, for the time being – builds into one of those quietly angry mobs you see from time to time on freshly landed planes.

"It must be French," Turnbull mutters, to no-one in particular.

Then he snaps back into the real world and notices a gentleman hovering tentatively at his right armpit. Accurately gauging his concern, Turnbull retrieves a suitcase from the overhead locker for the man and throws in a dazzling smile. The man looks utterly delighted.

Turnbull tends to switch on and off. You can be in an absorbing exchange with him and then notice that he has gone quiet, his conversational contribution reduced to the occasional sonorous "Mmmmm." Then you realise that he's twiddling away at the BlackBerry, or he's jammed the Bluetooth earpiece in his ear and is vetting phone messages.

Turnbull's fascination for gadgetry is boundless. He was an early enthusiast for information technology, and made a bundle when he and his buddy Trevor Kennedy sold their stake in OzEmail a decade ago. He is addicted to his BlackBerry, emails at all hours and is signed up to Facebook, Twitter and MySpace. He is constantly rifling through and making additions to his own electronic diary, to the consternation of his staff.

Turnbull can switch with deceptive ease between real communication and electronic communication. In the flight lounge in Hobart several hours earlier, I had plumped down in a seat next to him and asked if he would like a cup of tea – I was fetching one for myself.

Knitting his eyebrows and staring straight ahead, he replied sternly: "Well, I can't see how that could possibly work." Scanning his face for clues (perhaps he was a coffee man?) I noticed the flash of the busy Bluetooth device clipped to his ear, realised my error and stole away.

Real-life conversations with Malcolm Turnbull, however, are worth sticking around for. In Canberra, you are considered well-read if you've consumed everything on offer about Australian politics. If you've read about American and British politics as well, you are thought something of a don; knowledge of European politics implies the definite possibility that you might fancy yourself. Many, like John Howard, are voracious readers but restrict their consumption largely to their own professional field, with occasional excursions to the history shelves. Howard's ideal novel, one always suspected, would concern the policy adventures of a deeply principled, perhaps slightly built prime minister with a thing for cricket and an eagle-eyed wife.

Turnbull, however, has a taste for poetry and literature, and a tendency to veer away from politics at any and every conversational opportunity. When he called journalists together in December last year for Christmas drinks, we gathered in the Opposition party room under the framed photographs of his predecessors. Under such photos, most Christmases, do Opposition leaders deliver up a banal series of festive remarks along the lines that Christmas is the time for a brief ceasefire between the Opposition and the fourth estate, haw-haw.

Turnbull, who had by then been the leader of the Liberal Party for six weeks, eyed the photos briefly (tufty-browed Howard, soulful Brendan Nelson) and instead told a raucous story about Kerry Packer.

This one involved Packer hastily sticking a portrait of his father, Sir Frank, above his desk as a prop for an utterly fraudulent display of filial tears designed to extract more cash from Alan Bond for Channel Nine.

Once the Bond team was in his office and a figure mentioned for the sale, Packer commenced to gaze moistly at his father's portrait.

"When I look at my father and wonder what he'd think of my selling Nine ... well, I don't think he'd want me to do it," sniffled the mogul. When the Bond team was gone – having agreed to a fabulous price – Packer spun to face Turnbull and winked.

"Now, son – how'd that go?" he asked.

Turnbull confided to us that, deep down, he remained a journalist at heart. It was his first job. And he offered one piece of advice to the press gallery: "Don't be dull."

Turnbull himself has wasted very little of his life being dull, which is why conversations with him tend to be interesting. His life before politics has done several things for him. First, it's made him very rich. Second, it's made him some enemies. Third, it's given him an inexhaustible supply of dinner-party anecdotes.

"Malcolm is a colossal name-dropper," says one former cabinet colleague. "He won't just offer an opinion on economic policy – he'll always preface it with something like 'As I was saying to Tim Geithner the other day ...'"

Name-dropper, yes. But to be fair, he has excellent material. "Six Degrees of Malcolm Turnbull," in which any famous person in the world can be connected to Turnbull within six steps, would be a feasible party game. John F. Kennedy? Okay: from Kennedy we make an easy leap to his showbiz friend Frank Sinatra, and thence to Sinatra's fellow rat-packer Humphrey Bogart. Who starred in *Casablanca* with Ingrid Bergman, who was leading lady in *Gaslight*, which was also the screen debut in 1944 for a very young Angela Lansbury, whose cousin Coral ten years later gave birth to her first and only child, Malcolm Bligh Turnbull.

Mick Jagger? That's even easier. Jagger is a one-time guest of Brixton Prison, having been briefly incarcerated there in 1967 after police busted him with a modest quantity of illicit mood-enhancement pills. Another former Brixton prisoner is Malcolm Turnbull's great-great-uncle, the former British Labour leader George Lansbury. Lansbury, as Labour mayor of Poplar in 1921, did six weeks in Brixton as a penalty for redistributing council tax income to the needy rather than funnelling it to London; this heroic gesture produced the term "Poplarism" and transformed Lansbury into a folk hero.

Incidentally, Brixton wasn't the first stretch of stir for Turnbull's ancestor: George Lansbury was sent to Pentonville in 1913 for his impassioned speeches in defence of the Suffragettes and was only released after embarking upon a hunger strike.

He once shocked the House of Commons by shaking his fist in the face of Herbert Asquith, the Liberal British prime minister, who – just in case you're still playing "Six Degrees" – is the great-grandfather of the Hollywood actress Helena Bonham Carter.

Lansbury emigrated briefly to Australia in 1884 with his wife and three children, but was so horrified by the harsh conditions that he herded his family back to Britain and commenced a political campaign against the British authorities for distributing misleading propaganda to potential emigrants.

Lansbury's staunch pacifism (he remains the only major-party leader in Britain to have responded to the threat of war by calling for immediate, full disarmament) cost him dearly within the Labour Party and he eventually stood down as leader in 1935.

"Lansbury has been going about dressed in saint's clothes for years waiting for martyrdom," sneered his Labour colleague Ernest Bevin, who had precipitated Lansbury's resignation by denouncing him. "I set fire to the faggots."

For all his popularity and strength of principle, Lansbury never led the Labour Party to an election. The socialist writer Beatrice Webb, evaluating Lansbury's life and work, was driven regretfully to the conclusion that while he was a "great heart," he suffered from being an "emotional non-thinker." As so often happens in politics, the times did not suit him.

Malcolm Turnbull's life is full of recurrent themes, little refrains or trails of coincidence that add an extra sparkle to his unlikely biography. How apposite, for example, that Turnbull's great-great-uncle too should have found himself in a time of worldwide financial strife, leading a party with which he was out of step.

At times, the Turnbull life-story seems almost to have the silvery impermanence of cinema, and you suspect that somewhere behind it all is a haggard old-time Hollywood screenwriter, artfully inserting plot twists and complex little synchronicities for the benefit of the audience. The screenwriter (let's call him Irv) has relied, for the fundamentals, on a classic rags-to-riches theme.

Smart boy, not much dough, abandoned by his mother at eight, left alone a lot as a kid, sent to boarding school, loving but absent father, forced to rely on own brilliance. Brisk university life, period of feckless womanising, moonlights as brilliant young journalist, snapped up by grumpy tycoon. Rhodes scholar, famed barrister, fabulous clever wife, adorable family, filthy-rich banker, substantial philanthropist, stormed into parliament, breezed into cabinet, seized the Liberal leadership ... and that's as far as we've got.

Don't think that this is a mere fairy story, either; Irv's clearly worked with Orson Welles, for there's plenty of darkness too. Our hero is flawed: he is impatient and mercurial, and his life is littered with people who cannot forgive him his victories, feeling them ill-gotten. It's as though he has a poisoned sword. The wounds he has inflicted on others don't seem to go away; they tend to canker and are nursed bitterly by the injured, sometimes for years and years. Perhaps he's not a gracious winner; perhaps it's that. He certainly does not like to lose.

It was George Lansbury's outrage at the injustice of life in Australia that drove him into politics a century ago. His great-great-nephew took a more circuitous, if more spectacular, path. Unlike most practitioners, Malcolm Turnbull was not made famous by politics. He was famous already, having reaped abundant headlines as Kerry Packer's Boy Friday, as the cheeky advocate of the *Spycatcher* case, and as the captain of the doomed ship HMAS *Australian Republic*.

Turnbull was not, like some of his colleagues or indeed his own ancestor, driven to enter politics because of some galvanising injustice that nagged and fretted at him. He did not storm into politics to strike a blow for small business against Paul Keating, as many new Liberal MPs did in 1996. Quite the reverse; the mid-1990s found Malcolm Turnbull discussing, with various Labor figures including Keating, the prospect of his recruitment as a Labor parliamentarian. "Initiated by Keating!" protests Turnbull, who says he refused the approach. "Initiated by Turnbull!" insists Graham Richardson, who wrote that Turnbull asked him in 1993 for a Senate spot but legged it on being told about the tender delights of grass-roots ALP membership. When Turnbull finally did enter politics, it was to join a long-established Liberal incumbent, John Howard.

So what is he doing in politics? This is a question that has occupied colleagues and staffers in countless happy hours of speculation since his arrival in Canberra. Unlike John Howard, Malcolm Turnbull does not seem to be haunted by nameless inner cravings for major structural reform; the teenage Turnbull, one imagines, went to bed dreaming of one day becoming prime minister, while Howard's night-time reveries were complicated affairs in which he single-handedly dismantled Australia's system of centralised wage-fixing.

Turnbull was driven into politics partly by aptitude and ambition, partly by a sense of public service and partly, one suspects, by the gravitational pull of fate. "A force of nature" is how Tim Costello once described him, and this is a variation on an oft-repeated theme among colleagues, many of whom, from the moment of his nomination for the seat of Wentworth, have viewed Turnbull as a sort of galloping inevitability – something to be *got through*, like puberty or chickenpox.

Malcolm Turnbull's greatest moments to date have been as an advocate: a champion with a brief. Given a case to defend, be it Kerry Packer's innocence of the Goanna allegations before the Costigan Royal Commission, or Peter Wright's book *Spycatcher*, he is a giant-killer. Packer, with whom Turnbull had a relationship of intimate volatility, used him best of all. He directed Turnbull into negotiations where the young man's aggressiveness, and single-mindedness in pursuit of an outcome, were used to devastating effect. John Howard did something similar, in unleashing Turnbull on the rotten clubhouse of vested interests that is water management in Australia. In circumstances – like the republic referendum – where he is required to chart a direction for others to follow, Turnbull's results tend to be poorer.

As Opposition leader, Turnbull has flung himself daily at the decisions and pronouncements of the prime minister, and with a lawyer's zeal lays out the risks and flaws in the government's management of the financial crisis. He is eloquent and intelligent in his delivery. But nothing seems to be shifting in his favour; not the published polls, nor the parties' private research, which finds that people think Turnbull is negative, a carper.

Voters are not like jurors; they don't make a balanced decision on the basis of everything put before them. They look for a story, and Turnbull – at the moment – isn't giving them one. "He has a lawyer's intellect," says one former employee. "I have never seen anybody able to absorb information in the way that he does. But you never hear him talking about what the conceptual, thematic link is."

Paul Keating, that savage verbal caricaturist, said, "I fancy Malcolm is like the big red bunger. You light him up, there's a bit of a fizz, then nothing. Nothing."

How would Australia be different if he were prime minister? What are his most closely held policy convictions? I asked dozens of Malcolm Turnbull's political colleagues this question, asking them to name three. Many of them had to pause before responding.

"You'll have to excuse me. I'm eating some chocolate," was the best initial response, from a Liberal on the other end of a phone line.

But most made, as their first answer, mention in some way or other of the word "freedom." Chief among these was Turnbull himself: "I believe passionately in a free society, in government enabling people to do their best rather than telling them what's best. It's really a question of making sure that people have the maximum choice, that we have as much competition as possible and that we eliminate obstacles to starting a business and managing a business."

To this central tenet, Turnbull adds some specific policy interests, saying that "when I am prime minister, we will return to one of my policy fascinations, which is water and water management." He also says he wants Australia to repair its spotty record on innovation, describing the country's relative dearth of intellectual-property-based industries as "one of our greatest failures, for a highly educated country." Lastly, he mentions tax reform: "We've got to reward innovation more. Because the difficulty now is that people with innovative skills just go somewhere else."

Tax reform, or more precisely Turnbull's backbench championing of a 40 per cent top tax rate soon after he entered politics, is one of the reasons for the hostile relationship between Malcolm Turnbull and Peter Costello. Turnbull's campaign set the then treasurer's teeth on edge, and relations have not improved since.

John Howard's assessment of Turnbull's central policy convictions is as follows: "He does believe in market-centred economics. He does believe in as small a role for government as is appropriate given the circumstances

– I think he is quite genuine about that. And he does have a real understanding about the financial system. There aren't too many people who really understand it, and he's one of them. Peter Costello did, and I did, and I can't think of too many others. He is a stronger believer, he rests more ... I think he genuinely does buy the scientific arguments about the climate, more so than I did. His instincts in what one might call family issues I think are quite conservative. He's sort of quite a family-man type person. Our views on things like gay marriage are not that different, and he had an atypical electorate. He empathised with the gay community, which is fine. They are the three things that have always hit me."

Brendan Nelson plumps for: "Creating an environment that's conducive to business. The Jewish issues: Israel, and the Jewish community. And the third thing I've heard him talk about is strong views in support of the gay community. Things that are important to his electorate."

"He's very much what I would call a sort of British liberal," offers Alexander Downer. "He's sort of a 'live and let be' sort of person. John Howard was much more conservative in that respect. He was more of the view that the state had a special role to play in protecting people from themselves." Downer also mentions the liberal market model and climate change as central policy interests for Turnbull.

"Malcolm is an optimist," says George Brandis. "As he often says, he's in the Liberal Party because he thinks it's all about encouraging people to be the best they can be, not telling them what to be. One of the things I find striking about Malcolm is that he is essentially not a cynical person."

The writer Tom Keneally says Turnbull – with whom he has a warm if slightly scarred relationship dating back two decades to the birth of the Australian Republican Movement – is driven by a genuine feeling of obligation to spread his good fortune around.

"I always felt that he was, particularly in the late 1980s and early 1990s, a minority among the new rich in that he had the feelings of *noblesse oblige*," Keneally says. "He wouldn't be out of place as a Venetian Doge."

And there is indeed something of the Italian Renaissance about Turnbull, preposterous as that sounds. He and his wife Lucy are compulsive givers to charities, hospitals and church enterprises. Recently he handed a personal cheque for $50,000 to the Sydney Cancer Centre at a function, asking to remain anonymous (and this story did not come from Turnbull). He gave another $50,000 to charity at the 2007 Press Gallery Midwinter Ball. Most years, the Turnbulls give away somewhere in the region of half-a-million dollars. Turnbull is a patron of the arts, classically libertarian in his political tendencies and imbued with a passionate love of language. His sense of his own obligation to society is sincere, though at times you do have to smother a laugh.

"I felt the best thing I could do was to write a useful book about why Australia should be a republic," Turnbull wrote grandly in 1999, on the origins of his republican odyssey. "I made arrangements with my publisher, Sandy Grant. Then, in the manner of most authors, I became distracted with other matters."

The painter Lewis Miller was commissioned by Lucy and Malcolm Turnbull in 1994 to paint portraits of the family. Miller spent a week with the Turnbulls on their farm at Scone, where Turnbull's father is buried.

Miller chose to depict Malcolm and Lucy in close profile on two separate canvases, in the style of Piero della Francesca's famous diptych *The Duke and Duchess of Urbino*. In the background, rather than della Francesca's Marche landscapes, stretches the land around Scone.

The reference is a deliberate one. The Duke of Urbino – Federigo da Montefeltro, known as the "Light of Italy" – was a poetry-loving, library-building sort of cove, a giver of alms to the poor and a nurturer of young artists, among them the young Raphael. The Light of Italy and his wife, Battista Sforza, ruled together over Urbino in enviable private harmony; their relationship of equality (rare for the times, particularly when you consider that the Duchess married at thirteen) is reflected in the perfect symmetry of della Francesca's beautiful work.

It is easy to see how Miller was seized by his theme. There is no question, for instance, that Lucy Turnbull is the most important person in her husband's world (all right then, pedants: *second* most important). She has helped him with all the biggest deals of his life, not just as a supportive spouse but as a lawyer, businesswoman and politician in her own right. Turnbull constantly defers to his wife's judgment, citing her ceaselessly in conversation and even in shadow cabinet, where his "Lucy thinks ..." is a familiar refrain."I have a sense of us, rather than of me," he says. "I regret every minute I am not with her. We are very, very close – in some respects we are two individuals but also we are one entity."

Our scriptwriter's sense of humour was hilariously evident, in September last year, when Brendan Nelson announced that he would stand aside from the Liberal leadership and cause a ballot to be held. Turnbull was in – of all places – Venice. Lucy Turnbull was a commissioner of the 2008 Venice Architecture Biennale, and her husband attended as her handbag. This delicious detail allowed government ministers to address Turnbull for a time as "The Merchant of Venice" – a taunt so apt that it elicited a smile even from its target.

It should be noted as a postscript that Lewis Miller and Turnbull, the artist and patron, did not always see eye to eye. The portraits of the children – Alexander and Daisy – are still in the Turnbulls' Point Piper home, but the parents are nowhere to be seen: Malcolm and Lucy didn't like the paintings much. Miller recalls that he commenced another portrait of

Turnbull for the Archibald Prize in 1995, but Turnbull – shown the work in progress – did not like it and withdrew his cooperation. Turnbull registered his disapproval with the art dealer Ray Hughes, to whose gallery Lewis was at the time attached. According to Hughes, he ran into Turnbull at a book launch and was told: "That artist of yours is no good. He's made me look like a fat, greedy bastard."

"Well, Malcolm," rasped Hughes in delighted reply. "You must remember that he is a *realist* painter." Turnbull says he has no memory of the Archibald portrait, or the encounter with Hughes.

Malcolm Turnbull's life is full of little trailing creepers that lead tantalisingly off the terrain of Australian politics to more exotic destinations. Conversations with him are the same. One day we are talking about the Australian edition of the *Spectator* and whether it will last. Turnbull says he thinks it will (he is enthusiastic about new publications, as a rule, and wasn't fibbing when he said he retains a passion for journalism).

"I once tried to buy the *Spectator*," he adds, almost as an afterthought.

A furtive check reveals that, yes, he did. Charles Moore, editor of the *Spectator* from 1984 to 1990, wrote in 2003 about his encounter with Turnbull nearly twenty years earlier:

> One dark winter afternoon, I returned from parliament to my office and found Malcolm Turnbull sitting on the sofa. Turnbull was soon to become famous as the lawyer in the Spycatcher case, and, later, as one of the leaders of the unsuccessful republican movement in Australia, but at this time he was Kerry Packer's man of business, and I had never heard of him. He told me that Packer wanted to buy *Spectator* (he omitted the definite article) and that the deal would be through next week. I felt very depressed and asked Turnbull why Mr Packer wanted the paper. He thought for a moment and then said: 'Well, Kerry's not only motivated by greed.' He then seemed to reflect that he had done his boss an injustice, for he added: 'Well, not all the time, anyway.' Luckily, this coincided with the Goanna

Affair, a complicated scandal in Australia in which Mr Packer was somehow involved. As a result, the deal did not happen.

Four years later, according to Moore's account, he received a call from Rupert Murdoch.

"I've just been offered the *Spectator* by Malcolm Turnbull," the mogul announced.

"I hadn't realised it was Malcolm's to sell," grumped Moore, who in any event repelled Murdoch's advance. Turnbull, for his part, has no memory at all of trying to interest Murdoch in the magazine.

The *Spectator* episode gives us an insight into what Malcolm Turnbull was like in business. Speculative, confident, showy, and prepared to invoke names in order to further his own plans. When asked in detail about his *Spectator* bid, Turnbull can't quite remember if he had even been working for Packer at the time of his approach to Moore.

"I talked to Kerry about it; Kerry wasn't that interested," he recalls. "He was sort of mildly interested. It was only worth a million quid – not a lot of money. It was a fixer-upper. Not, in any conventional terms, a serious asset."

Then he is off into another fascinating reminiscence: from 1989, when he and Packer attempted to buy London's *The Times* and the *Sunday Times*, then owned by the Thomson Corporation and riven with industrial strife. Turnbull himself had been a first-hand veteran of the industrial trouble.

Here's the background: Turnbull, who travelled to Britain and the United States during his university holidays in late 1975, gave a speech at the Cambridge Union while he was there. After his oration, Turnbull was thrilled to receive a handwritten note from the famed *Sunday Times* editor Harold Evans (who, thanks to the magical hand of Fate that seems perennially to hover over Malcolm Turnbull, happened to be in the audience).

The note read: "Dear Turnbull – Magnificent speech. See me in the Gray's Inn Road tomorrow. Harold Evans."

"It was like a message from God," remembers Turnbull, who delivered himself smartly to *The Times'* famed London address the next day. Evans offered him a job on the spot; Turnbull demurred, saying he needed to go home and finish his law degree.

"Don't do law," Evans told him. "Terrible things could happen. You could become a judge. Or — worse — a politician!"

Turnbull did go home, but stayed in touch with Evans, and when he returned to England and Oxford in 1978 as a Rhodes scholar, he started work at the *Sunday Times*. But the paper was so mired in industrial discord that for ten months it was not published: Turnbull and the other hacks would spend the week running around writing stories that never saw the light of day because the print unions refused to print the paper. Good rehearsal for Opposition, perhaps, but hardly fun for a keen young journalist, so eventually Turnbull resigned and took himself back to Oxford to concentrate on his studies.

But he continued to think about what could be done to break the hold of the unions. And so to 1989. Turnbull had already worked for Kerry Packer as assistant to Packer's finance director, Harry Chester, for eight months (a heady experience for the young man that involved a trip to the *Playboy* mansion to negotiate an Australian edition of the soft-porn magazine). Now he thought that perhaps Packer could buy the *Times* group and introduce a union-busting plan that would get the papers back in print.

Packer, Turnbull and Evans (for the editor was receptive to the idea) staged some initial councils-of-war in Evans' Pimlico home.

"We had a Wapping plan to deal with the unions," Turnbull remembers. "We had a very funny meeting about it at the Dorchester Hotel, working through all the logistics of getting the paper into the country, printing and distributing it. We had these partners from Linklaters telling us about the provisions of these acts and so on, and Kerry was getting frustrated. He eventually said: 'Look. I'm driving the truck, right? With all the papers on the fucking back. We're coming off the ramp at the back of the building. There are all these picketers. I beep the horn. They don't get out of the way. So I lean out the window and I say, "Can you please get out of the way?" But they don't get out of the fucking way. So I drive the truck very slowly, and I run one over. What law covers me then?' And this partner from Linklaters, very pale, stammers: 'The law of m-m-m-murder!'"

It's an excellent story. Turnbull is telling it in a Comcar, which is driving us from Launceston (where he addressed a Jobs Forum) to Hobart (where he is due to address a dinner). It is a journey that is interrupted at one point by Turnbull's insistence that we veer off the highway to visit the old garrison town of Ross, to view its sandstone bridge, convict-built in 1836.

The telling of the *Spectator*/Harold Evans/*Sunday Times* tale takes us through the suburbs of Hobart and all the way to the kerb outside his hotel, where the car draws up and Turnbull gathers his things even as he concludes the tale of Packer and the strike-breakers. He delivers the punchline practically leaning through the window of the car, then clips the Bluetooth contraption to his ear and disappears into his hotel, where he will have half an hour to himself before his speech to the Australian Chamber of Commerce and Industry's annual dinner.

Politically, Australia is going through a very bland dietary phase at present, I think as I clamber out of the car and set about locating my own, sadly inferior hotel.

Malcolm Turnbull, in many ways, is the kind of prime minister you'd want Australia to have: clever, outrageous, fearless and interesting. By instinct, he is a discloser; you don't very often hear him engaging in the kind of psycho-babble that is the curse of modern politics, and of which Kevin Rudd is a master.

When he appeared solo on the ABC's *Q&A* program in September last year, Turnbull was witty, expansive and candid. When asked about Peter Costello, he did not employ the dreadful stock response about having the highest regard for his abilities, and so on. "He's always got a good word for me! Good old Peter," he chuckled, cheerfully confirming that there was "no love lost" with the former treasurer. John Howard, who was travelling in the United States at the time of the broadcast, watched the Q&A episode on a podcast in his Los Angeles hotel room. He rates it Turnbull's best performance to date.

Turnbull's colleagues sometimes talk about "Bad Malcolm" and "Good Malcolm." Good Malcolm is precisely the Malcolm who appeared on the Q&A program: charming, attentive and utterly engaging. Good Malcolm is careful to consult with his colleagues and reminds himself constantly that he must not be overbearing or dictatorial. Good Malcolm is tremendous fun. Bad Malcolm, however, can be anywhere on the scale from distant to vicious, none of it good. Bad Malcolm is well known for blowing up at his staff.

During the Tasmanian excursion, there were several points at which Turnbull wandered off alone along roadside verges or through car parks, Bluetooth earpiece in place, and paced about expostulating and waving his arms. At the time, I wondered what the locals made of the spectacle of their alternative prime minister apparently conducting a long and robust argument with himself. Later, I discovered that one of these conversations was a phone hook-up during which Turnbull shouted at his economics adviser, Paul Lindwall, about the small-business policy he was due to announce that night in Hobart. Lindwall, a former Costello staffer, resigned within weeks.

During the month of April, two other Turnbull staffers resigned: Lindwall's deputy Nick Chapman, and Turnbull's long-standing adviser Brad Burke, a trusted intimate who did not fall out with Turnbull but left to seek a quieter life in Brisbane working for the Liberal Lord Mayor, Campbell Newman. Turnbull – like Kevin Rudd – tends to exhaust his staff at a greater rate than the average politician. Many are drawn to Turnbull for the invigorating experience of working closely with a significant intellect; for some, it's too bruising an experience. Speech drafts deemed unsatisfactory, briefings deemed inadequate, too many engagements in the diary: these are triggers that regularly trip Bad Malcolm's temper, although such outbursts are sometimes followed by the contrite appearance of Good Malcolm. Bad Malcolm has a habitual note of bitter sarcasm that never fails to wound. One former employee remembers thinking that Turnbull didn't have much insight into his staff's capabilities.

"He wasn't really interested in the tools he had; he just worked to bully them into getting the job done. If they were inappropriate for the job, he'd just keep bashing them against a rock until they were finished."

"Malcolm's an egomaniac" is a criticism you hear pretty often. One has to be careful, in politics, with allegations of egomania. Often, those who make the allegation most loudly about Turnbull are those who suffer mildly from the complaint themselves. A psychiatrist might call this projection. A school child might put it more simply: "It takes one to know one."

"Nick Whitlam said to me once, 'You'll never get the republic up while you're led by that egomaniac,'" recalls Tom Keneally. "Well, I said: 'Ego-fucking-*maniac*?!'" This observation is punctuated by Keneally's unmistakeable cackle, which in this case wordlessly completes the joke (Whitlam himself is not entirely without ego).

In politics, complainants tend to universalise their grievances – their practice is lobbying, after all, and their trade the depiction of the subjective as objective. So, quite often, when a political detractor says of Malcolm Turnbull, "He never listens to anyone," one needs to exercise caution lest the truth of the narrator's experience boil down to something rather narrower, viz: "He never listens to *me*."

There is little doubt that Turnbull is an egotist, in the sense that he evaluates situations first with an eye to his own interests. Sometimes, this is true to a comical degree. On election night in 2007, John Howard watched his own removal from public office on live television at Kirribilli House. He had not been in much doubt of the result, and the verdict was clear pretty early in the evening. Those present, including Howard's first chief of staff in government, Grahame Morris, recollect that the night found him composed.

As the evening progressed, Howard asked his driver to take him on the short journey across the Sydney Harbour Bridge to the Wentworth Hotel, on Phillip Street. Howard had previously celebrated four election victories at the Wentworth, but on this night, from quite early on, it was filled with a sea of lachrymose Young Liberals comforting themselves with alcohol.

As Howard's car crossed the bridge, his mobile phone rang, and his recollection is that he answered it to find a jubilant Turnbull on the other end of the line. Turnbull was calling with the glad tidings that he had extended his margin in Wentworth. He also had some suggestions for Howard's speech.

It is in remembering this conversation that Howard's amused tolerance for Turnbull is most in evidence.

"He did ring me, yes, and the purpose of the call was to say something about himself," Howard grins. Turnbull is wounded at the thought that his call was construed as anything but a sympathetic attempt to reach out to the fallen leader.

"The fact of the matter was that I was moved by the sort of 'end-of-an-era' type of sense about it," he says. "I simply rang to say, you know, 'Keep your chin up, well done.' It was just a human reaction."

For a tough man, Turnbull is very vulnerable to slight. He is a great teller of anecdotes, and indulges happily in the modest embroidery that all good storytellers use to enhance and beautify their repertoires. But he does not enjoy anecdotes told by others in which he appears even faintly foolish. He has two responses to such stories, when confronted with them: Fight or Forget. Either he argues the toss about the exact circumstances of the anecdote itself, defending his own conduct as in the Howard phone call above, or he claims to have no memory of the incident whatsoever.

It is as if he cannot bear anyone else to draft a version of his history; it's no coincidence that he has written his own books about the *Spycatcher* case and the republic campaign, two of the most public chapters of his life.

Still, as Nietzsche wrote at the age of forty-two in his iconoclastic work *Beyond Good and Evil*, "egoism is the very essence of the noble soul." Or as Malcolm Turnbull (at nineteen) wrote in his student newspaper, *Honi Soit*: "One has to be somewhat egoistic to achieve anything, given the jealous, carping nature of the mass of humanity."

This grand pronouncement formed the third paragraph of an extremely grand 1974 article about Gough Whitlam by Turnbull, in which he suggested that the then prime minister had "fallen into the classic trap of the egomaniac." Whitlam had, posited the young Turnbull, surrounded himself with yes-men and as a result become out of touch. "This childish business of putting his leadership on the line every time he doesn't get his own way is straight out of the Elysée Palace in the days of de Gaulle," harrumphed the teenager. "Me or the wilderness? Well, de Gaulle said it once too often, for he had forgotten, in 1969, that everyone is dispensable. France and even the ALP will outlive their heroes of the moment." You get a pretty strong whiff here of what the student Turnbull might have been like – confident, opinionated, full of the heartbreaking assuredness of youth.

There is a difference between egoism and egotism; it's a slightly porous distinction and much-blurred by common usage, but certainly worth considering.

Egoism is a philosophical doctrine, subscribers to which believe that self-interest provides not only the motive for all conscious action, but the valid end of such action.

Egotism, on the other hand, is defined by Merriam-Webster as "excessive use of the first person singular personal pronoun" or "the practice of talking about oneself too much." Turnbull is certainly guilty of the second, but the first? That is a much harder call to make.

The business of the sudden switch-offs is something that colleagues do notice, and for his critics the irresistible conclusion is that Turnbull is only interested in one half of any conversation – his half. I suppose the most charitable explanation is that his considerable brain, like a shark, must remain in constant motion or perish.

The etymology of words is a particular fascination.

Turnbull tells a story over lunch one day about a visiting priest with whom he dined during the World Youth Day festival. "Pellegrino?" the waiter asked, and the priest ("*Si! Pellegrino!*") was thrilled to be so recognised.

"*Pellegrino*" means "pilgrim" in Italian. Somewhat deflatingly, however, it turned out that the waiter was merely offering him San Pellegrino fizzy water.

After telling the story, Turnbull is up out of his seat digging through his bookcase for the right dictionary, trying to find the origins of the word. He does this a lot; looking for quotations, considering correct usage. On another occasion, we are discussing a colleague and he springs up to find a Clive James poem that brilliantly encapsulates his feelings.

Turnbull has a merchant trader's smattering of languages, born of his business travel in the 1980s and 1990s and his innate fascination with words. He says that as a schoolboy he spoke "quite fluent, but vilely accented" French. In conversation, he regularly uses Yiddish expressions. And he did deliver a short speech in Russian several years ago, at the Russian Jewish community's Hanukkah celebration on Bondi Beach.

"How wonderful it is to be here, rather than at the beach resort of Odessa," he began his remarks, as Russian speakers in the crowd laughed and local officials looked puzzled. Not content simply with speaking Russian, Turnbull then executed an ambitious inside joke. "The wonderful thing about Bondi, as opposed to Odessa, is that you can be confident that all your personal belongings will be safe!" he said, facetiously – and still in Russian. The joke, which would have been comprehensible only to a Russian speaker familiar with both Bondi and Odessa, is that you are roughly 100 per cent likely to have your bag nicked at Bondi if you are ever so incautious as to leave it unguarded for a millisecond.

There's something magpie-like about Malcolm Turnbull. He collects fascinating bits of information, shiny little anecdotes, and has a prodigious mental store of detail in the policy areas which interest him. The technical detail of reforestation, carbon abatement and – more recently – the innovation of biochar is a playground of fascination for him.

While conducting a routine Coalition meeting on the government's carbon-sink legislation last year, Turnbull asked his colleagues: "Now: what about *Eucalyptus globulus*?" Barnaby Joyce, Turnbull's National Party nemesis, called out: "Why don't you just say 'bluegum,' Malcolm?" Turnbull simply raised his eyebrows and moved on, calling next for a discussion of "*Toona australis*." Joyce interrupted again: "If you mean the red cedar, I think you'll find its new scientific name is actually '*Toona ciliata*.'" Turnbull said nothing, but soon was observed stabbing away furtively at the BlackBerry, which thanks to the miracle of communications in the modern age must swiftly have delivered the disappointing news that Joyce was in fact correct.

This story is told – not without wry affection – by one who was present. But Turnbull, when I mention the anecdote, is indignant; his "Fight" impulse sets in. He resents the idea that he is thought pretentious for using Latin names for trees. "You see, if you talk about trees a lot," he insists, "one of the difficulties is that the common names of trees vary from place to place. A swamp oak in one place might be called something different in another area. A mountain ash, or *Eucalyptus regnans*, which is called a mountain ash in Victoria, is called something different in Tasmania. Take the sugar gum, *Eucalyptus cladocalyx* ..." Turnbull continues in this vein for some minutes, piling detail upon detail, until, of the original small funny story, little remains visible.

Turnbull has many gifts, but one of the most useful must surely be his ability to inject energy and enthusiasm into a room. In Launceston, he knocks over three radio interviews early in the morning and then arrives at the city's new Australian Technical College (one of the final innovations of the Howard government, now undergoing targeted extermination by Julia Gillard).

The building is a fabulous open-plan confection of polished concrete and stripy orange ceiling tiles. Its irreproachably modern interior, on this day, is crawling with young people learning how to plane things, or slicing freshly baked brownies at bold angles. But the room selected for Turnbull's Jobs Forum is a poor one, buzzing with background noise. And the crowd that awaits is not promising, consisting of about two dozen resigned-looking teenagers and perhaps a dozen local business people.

One of them, Peter Brohier, has extremely strong views about the pricing system on the ferry link to the mainland. Mr Brohier has a press release prepared (always an ominous sign) which proclaims that he was once described by former premier Paul Lennon as "the person most responsible for the introduction of the federal Bass Strait Passenger Vehicle Equalisation Scheme (BSPVES)."

In the movie *When Harry Met Sally*, Meg Ryan's character, still hankering after her ex-boyfriend Billy Crystal, probes her best friend Carrie Fisher about Crystal's new love interest. "What's she like?" Ryan asks, and Fisher responds, perfectly laconic: "Thin. Pretty. Big tits. Your basic nightmare."

Well – this room, with its noise, its special-interest delegates and its disengaged youth – is your basic nightmare for a politician. All that is missing is the person with a complicated Family Court case to discuss.

But Turnbull is seriously good at this stuff. His resonant voice drowns out the background noise. He listens good-humouredly to Brohier, and elicits questions even from the ranks of the teenagers, who clearly have attended under duress but after a while show every sign of real interest.

At the end of the session, one ponytailed girl – she is perhaps fifteen – raises her hand diffidently and catches Turnbull's attention.

"I live in Bridgeport, and I had to move to Launceston to go to school," she says, in a tremulous voice. "When I go to university, I'll probably have to move to the mainland. It's really hard to have to leave home. Can the government do anything to make it easier?"

Turnbull's face undergoes a queer rearrangement; a mixture of empathy, pain and nostalgia dances across his features.

"Well, you don't want to make growing up too easy, do you?" he says, awkwardly. As the audience laughs, he recovers his balance and tells the girl: "From the moment you leave your mother's womb, you leave a position of warmth and quiet and you come screaming and squalling into the world. But I have to say, there isn't a grown-up in this room who doesn't look at you and see what an exciting time you have ahead of you and wish that we were your age again. Don't be daunted."

Afterwards, Turnbull remains devastated by the girl's question; by its heartbreaking vulnerability and trust.

"What could I say? What can you say?" he exclaims, waving his arms. "I didn't even want to say anything – oh, I just wanted to burst into tears." His eyes, alarmingly, are filling with tears even as he remembers the girl. For all his toughness, Turnbull is extraordinarily susceptible to pathos.

To change the subject, he whips out his BlackBerry.

"Do you want to see something funny?" He scrolls through the device intently for a minute. "Here – I call this the Madame Bonaparte shot!" It's a picture of Lucy Turnbull, reclining on a couch majestically, with two terriers perched alertly on her hip and shoulder. She looks regally beautiful, and Turnbull holds the device back at arm's length, squinting proudly. "Can you imagine – looking like that at fifty?"

Not all Liberal MPs went to university. In fact, over the course of the Howard era it became a distinct advantage not to have been to university. But those Liberal MPs who edged into student politics and thence found themselves swept into the powerful currents of grown-up politics tended to have very different university lives from the one lived by Malcolm Turnbull.

Here's John Howard, for instance, speaking about his university years: "I was fairly non-involved at the university. I just did my course. When I was at university, I had a lot of trouble with my hearing. I wore a hearing aid for about eighteen months and I think that had a slightly inhibiting effect. That partly explains my lack of involvement in extra-curricular affairs. I tended just to be involved in study and in playing sport at the weekend."

Turnbull, however, found so much time for extra-curricular activities that he seemed often at grave risk of abandoning the academic experiment altogether. While studying arts and law at the University of Sydney from 1973, Turnbull worked freelance for, as he put it, "a leftish weekly called *Nation Review*." By 1976, he had managed to install himself in the NSW parliamentary press gallery and, while playing hookey from his university studies, filed reports for *Nation Review*, for the Catholic Church-owned radio station 2SM, and for Kerry Packer's Channel Nine. As he put it: "I was serving, simultaneously, Marx, God and Mammon."

Turnbull supplemented these income streams by flogging jingles to John Singleton, the adman who in 1977 introduced the young Turnbull to Kerry Francis Bullmore Packer. Already something of an entrepreneur, Turnbull dealt with the consequent traffic jam of demands on his time by outsourcing what he could.

At the reasonable rate of thirty dollars a week plus expenses, he hired a friend, John O'Sullivan, to attend lectures and take notes for him.

The mid-'70s were turbulent years on campuses around Australia. As

Turnbull began his university career, Liberal students busied themselves with outrages against the Whitlam government or fought Trotskyists in the unique cublike rough-and-tumble that constitutes university politics. When Whitlam was dismissed, a sizeable protest was staged against the governor-general, Sir John Kerr, at the University of New South Wales. Tony Abbott, an irreverent young conservative from the University of Sydney, promptly organised a pro-Kerr rally.

In Melbourne, a young Peter Costello and his friend Michael Kroger were caught up in a physical mêlée when the new prime minister, Malcolm Fraser, visited Monash University in 1975. Later, Costello was thumped by a campus Trotskyist in a crucial rite of passage. Eighteen days before the Whitlam government was dismissed in 1975, Turnbull celebrated a milestone birthday. "In response to popular demand, Malcolm Turnbull is turning twenty-one," the party invitations read.

Turnbull seemed to be on a different course. He developed a fascination with the ancient, poisonous and anti-Semitic figure of Jack Lang, the former Labor premier of New South Wales. During his first year at university, Turnbull regularly took a tape recorder and toiled up to the little Nithsdale Street office where Lang published his newspaper, the *Century*, until well into his tenth decade.

Turnbull, with his unreliable tape recorder, was there not just to soak up Lang's peppery epithets. Bizarrely enough, he was planning to write a musical about Lang, in collaboration with the leftist writer Bob Ellis.

"I was already a well-known writer by then," says Ellis of their meeting in about 1973. "I had a girlfriend who I lost, and she turned up again with Malcolm about eighteen months after she left me, and to my chagrin I got to like him. He seemed roughly like he does now, which is a kind of somewhat naive and likeable and driven but essentially shy sort of fellow. We then used to go out rooting, and we would find ourselves alternatively in the same beds with different women and so on."

The musical was to have been called *Lang Is Right!* The project itself – perhaps unsurprisingly – collapsed, and never made it to the stage.

"The whole purpose of all the taping was to write this damn thing, but I was of course egocentric and always doing other things," says Ellis. "Eventually he came around to discuss the play and I didn't want to see him, and so told him to fuck off. He broke the door down and raged at us till dawn, which intervention caused us to move to the northern beaches."

The tapes of Turnbull and Lang's conversations survive, somewhere inside Malcolm and Lucy Turnbull's house.

Of the musical, not much remains. Turnbull says at first that he might still have it. A couple of weeks later, he sends an email to pronounce it lost. But Ellis says he retains a scrap or two, and produces one scene in which Adolf Hitler appears before a group of "fat capitalists." Hitler comes across as trenchant, with a hint of camp (although in fairness this might just be the format).

> You who are men of high and lofty station
> Of noble birth and high school education
> With families full of generals, kings and princes
> I could hardly expect you to know where Linz is.

He is seeking liquidity:

> Tonight I will not ask for much; just a short solicitation;
> Ten million marks, your blessing, and your kind co-operation ...
> My way of doing business may not appeal to you;
> But tread softly lest you find yourself included with the Jew.

The refrain imparts an almost danceable feel:

> Just a little one step, two step, three step,
> Just a little goose step, four;
> Just a little bit of "Heil, Mein Führer"
> Just a little bit of war.

When I read these snippets out to Turnbull, he laughs and insists that they were not part of the musical.

"God, no. Hitler did not make an appearance. Bob must be mixed up," he says. "I do remember that there was this dreadful line, set in McNamara's Bookshop where Lang met his wife, that rhymed 'Patagonia' with 'new Australian utopia.' It was terrible."

The Hitler verses are in Turnbull's handwriting; they match another memento in Ellis's collection, a little poem titled "A Song, by Malcolm Turnbull." Are they part of the Lang musical? Ellis thinks so. But Ellis has been wrong before, and Turnbull says he doesn't remember them at all.

"I remember at one point there was this marvellous exchange," says Ellis, who listened to some of the tapes of the teenager and the old man, "where you can hear Lang saying sharply, 'What do you mean? What do you mean it's not going?' And Malcolm, who's fiddling with the tape, says, 'I think it's all right.' And Lang barks: 'My time's valuable!'"

A digression here is warranted to note that Lang is Right! was by no means Turnbull's only stab at the poetry game. He won, in 1974, the University of Sydney poetry prize named for Henry Lawson, who (thanks, Irv!) happened to be Jack Lang's brother-in-law.

Turnbull's winning entry was a dreadful piece of doggerel entitled "A Woman is Just a Woman, But a Good Cigar is a Smoke." Turnbull wrote the poem as a speech for a debate on the topic of the title and garnered such an uproarious reception that he submitted it for the Lawson Prize and won.

The poem spins the yarn of an outback pub called the Golden Bandicoot, whose publican, Sam McPhee, discovers that when the drovers come in from months of isolation, it is not the company of the fairer sex that they crave, but the hot blast of a fine cigar.

> So he spurred up his horse and rode like the wind for the 'Golden Bandicoot'
> And hoped that he'd soon be wrapping his lips round a smouldering fat cheroot.
> He leapt off his horse and burst like a shell through the hotel's swinging door,
> Fixed Sam McPhee with a madman's gaze, "you know what I've come here for."

Looking back, Turnbull remembers his mother being horrified that he should win the Henry Lawson Prize with such a romp. She had won it herself back in the 1940s, she told him, for a far more worthy work.

The subject of Australia's most successful political musical, Paul Keating, was another adherent of Lang. Keating was a teenage haunter of the Century office ten years before Turnbull, and in 1971 campaigned successfully to have Lang, then ninety-five, readmitted to the Labor Party.

"What it was that drew them to the rancorous old mountebank, then in his nineties, and his endless festering defamations of the dead, may lie in their similar souls and in their similar teenage dreams of rapid glory," wrote Ellis of Turnbull and Keating's shared fascination in a piece for the ABC website *Unleashed*, in late 2008.

"In Lang's bellowing monomania, his rancid certitude, his boofheaded political martyrdom, his Catholic nepotistic tribalism, his messianic, hectoring style they found, I guess, as young men do, a pleasing role model, a Labor legend to follow like a pillar of fire through the wilderness of this world to, yes, a political martyrdom of their own."

Turnbull does seem to have had a natural fascination for difficult political martyrs: he travelled to Britain while at university and interviewed Enoch Powell, the former Conservative MP and fiery orator who was sacked from the party's front bench in 1968 after his infamous "Rivers of Blood" speech about race relations. Continuing to America on the same trip, he tried to interview the disgraced Richard Nixon but had no luck. Turnbull himself tells the story about his conversation with Neville Wran, shortly after Wran was convicted for contempt of court in 1987. Wran, at a press conference, had expressed his belief in the innocence of his friend, the then High Court Justice Lionel Murphy, who was at the time about to undergo retrial on charges of perverting the course of justice (he was later acquitted of all charges). Wran was convicted for contempt and fined $25,000; Turnbull, outraged, offered to undertake a legal appeal for his mentor.

"I'll pay the fine," Wran told him. "The Labor Party loves a martyr."

Mark Latham, federal Labor's short-lived leader of 2003 and 2004, also found much to admire in Lang, and published an article on him in 1992 with the collaboration of Lang's son, Chris.

"For all his firebrand ways and capacity of stirring trouble within the ALP, Lang merely used the tools available to him to maximum effect as a politician," wrote Latham, in whose violent political tactics more than a sniff of Langishness was evident. "In public life it was ever thus."

Turnbull, who wrote an obituary of Lang in 1975 for the *Nation Review*, seemed similarly drawn to Lang's "whatever it takes" approach.

"Once premier, Lang showed himself to be totally ruthless in his efforts to secure the passage of Labor legislation," Turnbull wrote. "He had always been convinced that the end justified the means and recalled with pride how, in 1916, he contributed to the defeat of the conscription referendum by inventing the rumour that Hughes planned to import thousands of Chinese coolies to do the work of the Australians conscripted to fight in France."

But the grandest of Lang's suicidal gestures, of course, and the trigger for his eventual dismissal, is found in the great dispute of the early 1930s over his repudiation of NSW's crippling interest payments to Britain. In order to evade court orders from the Commonwealth, Lang instructed his public servants to collect the state's revenues in cash. He barricaded the state treasury and set unemployed timber workers to guard it, vowing to spend his state's money on the poor of New South Wales, not the wealthy of London.

Lang went down, but there is a throb of heroism in his tactics that yet causes certain hearts to beat faster. The fact that Lang's tactics so closely mirrored those of Malcolm Turnbull's own maternal great-great-uncle (handing out taxes as alms comes straight from the Poplarist playbook) might explain some of Malcolm Turnbull's interest.

Certainly, he seemed very taken with Lang. "If Lang's depression politics appear wild and misguided, it is only because of the comparison with the 'safe' and inhumanly cautious policies of the other governments of the day," argued the young Turnbull in his obituary for the *Nation Review*. "Like Roosevelt, Oswald Mosley and even Hitler, Lang was advocating, ahead of his time, reflationist solutions to the depression."

Thin ice, this. And very much indicative of the old man's force of personality. A few afternoons in Lang's company and you're already thinking, well, Hitler may have been a bastard, but he had some good economic policies. Elsewhere in the obituary, explaining Lang's equivocal relationship with capitalism, Turnbull neutrally mentions Lang's belief that "the wealthy Jews of London, through their control of the Bank of England, dominated and manipulated the Australian banks."

It's hard to imagine the grown-up Turnbull — who is a passionate supporter of the state of Israel and boasts extensive networks in the Jewish community — taking that one lying down.

The grown-up Turnbull is in many respects far more cautious about Lang.

"He was a very colourful personality and he was larger than life in every respect," he ventures, in defence of his early interest. "He was also alive — apart from Bill McKell, there were no other politicians from the 1920s who were still around. He was filled with vituperation and venom. I wouldn't ever have wanted to have one zillionth of his bitterness.

"As my understanding of that period developed, and I talked to McKell, I really accepted his view eventually that Lang was a bit of a coward."

We cannot conclude any discussion of Turnbull's early years without visiting an incident which has trailed him unshakeably all the way through his eventful life. To friend and foe alike, the story is known simply as "The Cat."

"The Cat" has many functions. In the hands of some narrators, it's allegory. In others, it's pure fable. There are people who will swear blind that it is fact. And it serves as a rough indicator of general opinion on Turnbull.

So what are the facts, in the case of The People v Malcolm Turnbull (*ex parte* The Cat)? Turnbull, in about 1977 — before he met Lucy — knocked

Never again miss an issue. Subscribe and save.

1 year subscription (4 issues) only $49 (incl. GST). Subscriptions outside Australia $79.
All prices include postage and handling.

2 year subscription (8 issues) $95 (incl. GST). Subscriptions outside Australia $155.
All prices include postage and handling.

PAYMENT DETAILS Enclose a cheque/money order made out to Schwartz Media Pty Ltd.
Or; Please debit my credit card (Mastercard, Visa Card or Bankcard accepted).

CARD NO.

EXPIRY DATE   /   AMOUNT $

CARDHOLDER'S NAME

SIGNATURE

NAME

ADDRESS

EMAIL   PHONE

freecall: 1800 077 514 **fax:** 61 3 9654 2290 **email:** subscribe@blackincbooks.com **www.quarterlyessay.com**

An inspired gift. Subscribe a friend.

1 year subscription (4 issues) only $49 (incl. GST). Subscriptions outside Australia $79.
All prices include postage and handling.

2 year subscription (8 issues) $95 (incl. GST). Subscriptions outside Australia $155.
All prices include postage and handling.

PAYMENT DETAILS Enclose a cheque/money order made out to Schwartz Media Pty Ltd.
Or; Please debit my credit card (Mastercard, Visa Card or Bankcard accepted).

CARD NO.

EXPIRY DATE   /   AMOUNT $

CARDHOLDER'S NAME   SIGNATURE

ADDRESS

EMAIL   PHONE

RECIPIENT'S NAME

RECIPIENT'S ADDRESS

freecall: 1800 077 514 **fax:** 61 3 9654 2290 **email:** subscribe@blackincbooks.com **www.quarterlyessay.com**

Delivery Address:
Level 5
289 Flinders Lane
MELBOURNE VIC 3000

No stamp required
if posted in Australia

Quarterly Essay
Reply Paid 79448
MELBOURNE   VIC   3000

Delivery Address:
Level 5
289 Flinders Lane
MELBOURNE VIC 3000

No stamp required
if posted in Australia

Quarterly Essay
Reply Paid 79448
MELBOURNE   VIC   3000

around with a young woman by the name of Fiona Watson, who lived in a tiny single-storey terrace in Double Bay. She was a remarkably beautiful young woman, and the young Turnbull was besotted with her. To complicate matters, or possibly to enhance them, she was the stepdaughter of the Labor senator and wit "Diamond" Jim McClelland, being the daughter of McClelland's second wife, Freda Watson, whom McClelland wed in 1968.

By all accounts it was a turbulent relationship, and for reasons that are now lost to us, Miss Watson decided to end it; she had no shortage of suitors. Turnbull, who even then was not one to accept defeat lightly, embarked upon a passionate letter-writing campaign directed at Miss Watson's cat, an animal of which she was inordinately fond. In the letters, Turnbull exhorts the beast to intercede with its mistress and convince her to take him back. As a romantic technique, it errs toward the Elizabethan. But who are we, after all these years, to question the epistolary methods of a young man who has lost his girl? The real intrigue set in later, when Miss Watson arrived home one day to find the cat, dead, outside her house.

No evidence exists to connect Malcolm Turnbull with the fatality, beyond the letters (which establish some degree of emotional engagement with the creature) and some circumstantial murmurings from the neighbours to the effect that he had been seen hanging round in the weeks preceding. It's not a prosecution that any sensible lawyer would attempt. But the rumour that Turnbull had strangled the cat quickly gained currency — particularly among the legal community, where, thanks to his impertinent weekly *Bulletin* column on matters of the law, Turnbull was thought something of an upstart.

In 1981, the *National Times* published a small gossip item by Richard Ackland, who in the course of some observations about Mr Turnbull's candidacy for Liberal preselection in the federal seat of Wentworth, wondered archly what the cat-lovers would make of him. Mr Turnbull's writ arrived very quickly, and after a hurried pow-wow involving Miss Watson, Mr Ackland and the Fairfax-retained barrister Neil McPhee, the matter was settled in Mr Turnbull's favour, with modest damages. Several years later, another Fairfax columnist was incautious enough to add the sobriquet "Cat Strangler" to Turnbull's name in print.

Again, Turnbull intervened quickly and secured a settlement. The matter has never been to court, and the speed of the settlements suggests that it never will; as a cold case, the whole thing is pretty hopeless.

Conrad Black, the Canadian media magnate, repeated the rumour in his autobiography, *A Life In Progress*. (*A Life In Progress*, it must be remembered, is a work published in 1993, which was well before Mr Black's life progressed as far as his current residential address, Florida's Coleman Federal Correction Complex, where he is serving six years for fraud and goes by the name Inmate 18330-424). The book's Australian edition restrains itself to the prim recollection that "Malcolm's fugues were notorious, such as the time (as a young single man) he allegedly punctuated an altercation with a friend by disposing of her cat." The version in the book's American edition, however, is so wildly inaccurate that it demonstrates just how intricate the embroidery of this tale has become.

"Malcolm's fugues were notorious," reads the unbowdlerised account enjoyed by residents of the more permissive defamation code in the United States of America. "Such as the time he allegedly punctuated an altercation with a friend by sneaking into her home late at night and putting her kitten into the freezer, transforming a frisky pet into a well-preserved corpse."

Meanwhile, over the years the cat has assumed a legendary status far in excess of its humble breeding. Last year, the departing *Sydney Morning Herald* columnist Alan Ramsey (one hesitates to use the word "retiring" of Ramsey, even when referring to a point in time at which the application of the term was technically warranted), used one of his final columns to present a cautious version of "The Cat."

Ramsey quoted from the for-Australian-eyes edition of Black's book, and cited his artist colleague Ward O'Neill's drawing of Turnbull during his 2004 struggle for the seat of Wentworth.

"It showed Turnbull in his dressing gown holding a coffee mug bearing the image of a cat, with a cat rubbing affectionately against his leg. Political aficionados with long memories understood," Ramsey recalled.

Businesspeople and journalists understood, too. Among Turnbull's army of detractors in Sydney, the cat story is retold with varying degrees of hysterical exaggeration. It functions as a kind of identifying mark. Much as you can tell whether your conversation partner is Labor or Liberal according to whether they refer to the "$42 billion stimulus package" or the "$42 billion cash splash," you know exactly where they stand on Turnbull depending on whether they try to tell you the story.

"The Cat" became a piece of eastern-suburban folklore. When Turnbull represented Packer through the "Goanna" affair, the satirist Max Gillies appeared as Packer, with a stocking pulled over his head; his routine contained a reference to cats, which would have made sense only to the initiated.

"Perhaps ... Malcolm is really a pussycat," mused the broadcaster Phillip Adams, in a 1991 profile of Turnbull.

At Fairfax, Turnbull's early hypersensitivity has given the story an untouchable status as one that cannot even be mentioned without inviting a "QCs at dawn"-style shootout. As I prepare to ask Turnbull about it, I wonder if he will fly into a rage or call in a lawyer. To my surprise, he laughs.

"All completely untrue!" he insists. "No cat has died at my hands."

Turnbull says he remembers the cat, which he thinks "got run over by a car. Someone, either maliciously or in jest, started the rumour and it was one of those things – sometimes the most outrageous and false things get the most currency." He says he cannot remember writing any letters, but does remember the rumours spreading quickly. "At the time, I was working at the Bulletin. I was very upset about it. I regard it as a joke now."

Turnbull further recalls that Trevor Kennedy, his editor at the time, extended him some blokey reassurance. Kennedy, who used to trap rabbits as a kid, had had occasion to dispatch feral cats that found their way into his traps.

"They're buggers – they scratch you all over the place," Turnbull remembers him saying. Having noticed no such scratches on Turnbull's arms, Kennedy offered his services as an expert witness should the need arise.

A postscript: the episode earned Turnbull, one way or another, the lasting hatred of the late Jim McClelland, who in 1991 had this to say of Turnbull: "He's a turd. He's easy to loathe, he's a shit, he'd devour anyone for breakfast, he's on the make, he's cynical, he's offensively smug." Turnbull shrugged at the time that McClelland was "a bitter old man ... I'm very sorry that many years of excessive consumption of alcohol and professional disappointment have reduced what was once a sharp wit to nothing better than gutter abuse," he told the writer Jonathan Lyons.

WHY DO THEY HATE ME?

That there are people who hate Turnbull is beyond doubt. "The Cat" is by no means the only yarn about him going around; it's just the most widely circulated. The rest of them tend to involve Turnbull's hairy-chested negotiating style, which has in the past included the throwing or threatened throwing of projectiles. His style of negotiation is certainly a memorable one: he never gives in, even on small details, and he will argue and wheedle and storm and bully until the other party either gives in or goes away. When in business, he dispensed legal threats like confetti.

Other threats, too, from time to time. During the frenzied negotiations in 1987 over the sale of Nine to Alan Bond, Turnbull found himself toe-to-toe with the Blake Dawson partner Bill Conley, who was acting for Bond. After Bond and Packer's handshake deal, it was left to the lawyers to argue about the sale's precise terms and conditions, in a ludicrously short period of time. Negotiations grew vexed and an angry Turnbull suggested that he and Conley "settle this outside."

Conley confirms the incident, but says he considered it minor – none of them had slept, he recalls, and tense moments occur in most big deals. "When you know the whole Malcolm, you're not going to be offended by his strong and direct way of dealing." The two men are friends, and Conley says he admires Malcolm and Lucy Turnbull's philanthropy. "Unlike some, they do not seek particular recognition but give because of their values," he says.

Tom Keneally, who received what you might call first-degree burns from Turnbull's temper when the two were thrown together during the republican debate, nevertheless remains fascinated by and fond of Turnbull.

"I've got a thing for difficult pricks, so I kind of on balance approve hugely of people like Malcolm and Germaine Greer, who have some similarities," says Keneally. "He bore fools very badly when he was younger, including myself – he was very abrasive." Keneally is a rare breed: one who has seen something of Bad Malcolm and maintains warm feelings.

Keneally is sympathetic towards the scalded ones: "Oh yes, absolutely. Though I've got to say it's not all his fault. It's also their own vulnerability. But yeah, I can understand why their reaction was like that. It was the abrasiveness, it was the knowledge – whether they saw it as smart aleckry, it was the acerbic turn of phrase. All that stuff. The word that was always used was 'arrogant.' And yet, I never thought of that adjective in my head. Hand on heart, I never thought of him as arrogant. I would have thought of other words – urgent, gifted, to an extent inspired. But Australia's a bad place to be inspired in."

If some people hate Malcolm Turnbull, who or what does Malcolm Turnbull hate? He is not particularly tribal, politically. How could he be, and keep a straight face? He has had as many Labor friends as Liberal, and many's the Labor voter I know who can't quite locate anything on which they disagree with Turnbull.

But it's deeper than that – Turnbull, for all his notorious rages and impatience, does not appear to be driven by hate. And his reaction to people who hate him isn't automatically to hate in return. It's something else entirely; something more like puzzlement.

"He's not obsessed with revenge the way nearly everybody is," is Bob Ellis's view. "He believes that he's given talents and called to service and is amazed that people can't see why he's the one."

A small example: in 1999, when the republican debate occupied a great deal of Canberra's brain, and Liberal MPs sorted themselves into piles marked "Yes," "No," and "Above the Fray," the Liberal Member for Parramatta, Ross Cameron, was in no doubt about which pile was his. Cameron was a monarchist, and he despised the Australian Republican Movement and by extension its lustrous leader, Malcolm Turnbull.

"The Turnbull-ARM republic we are being offered is a sop to our popular instincts," he told parliament on 30 August 1999. "It is a throwing of the scraps of democracy from the table of the elites. This is a 'We know better than you' republic."

Only days after getting this off his chest, Cameron found himself in a sticky situation of an entirely unconnected nature. As a member of parliament's prayer group, he had organised for a small group of young Aboriginal people to visit Canberra for a few days. Flights were booked, and the $5000 sponsorship from some anonymous businessman nailed down – or so Cameron thought.

At the last minute, his sponsor called to cancel the arrangement – disaster! This left Cameron in a spot, as he explained to his squash partner, Joe Hockey, over a morning game.

Hockey, a garrulous type who specialises in bringing together the needy and the benevolent, had an idea. After their showers, the pair convened in Hockey's office, where Hockey dialled Malcolm Turnbull's number.

Turnbull and Hockey were already friends. They'd met years before while Hockey was working on privatisations for the Fahey government in New South Wales. A young, friendly man with influence over large privatisation processes was, of course, of great interest to Malcolm Turnbull at that time, and the pair got to know each other well.

When Hockey's first child was born – a son, Xavier – Turnbull came to visit bringing a teddy bear in which a tiny tape recorder was implanted. When you pressed the bear's paw, Turnbull's voice issued forth: "Uncle Malcolm says, don't forget to vote Liberal!"

When Hockey telephoned for help with Cameron's little problem, Turnbull listened.

"Cameron? Ross Cameron? Isn't he the guy who just bagged me in parliament?"

Hockey put his hand over the phone. "Did you bag Malcolm Turnbull in parliament?" he whispered to the Member for Parramatta.

Cameron looked uncomfortable – "Weee-llllll …"

Hockey returned to the phone. "Come on, Malcolm. Have a heart?"

Turnbull laughed, stumped up the money and the trip went ahead.

This is not to say that Turnbull isn't prepared to use nuclear force against anyone who seeks to thwart him. He is – as even a cursory examination of his business and legal record makes amply clear. Bill Conley argues that Turnbull's benign attributes – generosity, charm and intelligence – make up for the flashes of anger. The problem is that Turnbull does business at such a breakneck rate that sometimes the brutality is all people get to see.

Breaking the Rules: Costigan

In late 1982, soon after the unexpected death of Turnbull's father, Bruce, in a light-plane accident, Turnbull agreed to go and work for Kerry Packer full-time as Consolidated Press's lawyer. Dazed by his father's death and faced with the task of settling his affairs, Turnbull thought in-house work would give him a more sedate lifestyle than that on offer at the Bar. But shortly after he started at Consolidated Press, he found himself defending Packer against the most vaporous of opponents. The Costigan Royal Commission, convened to investigate some rather colourful irregularities within the Federated Ship Painters and Dockers Union, began to hear evidence in secret about a well-known Australian businessman and his alleged involvement in drug running, pornography and murder.

In 1984, the *National Times* published sensational case summaries from the commission, including one concerning the mystery businessman. The newspaper gave the businessman an evocative nickname: "The Goanna." Speculation about the identity of the Goanna was rife: "Packer Is The Goanna" read a piece of graffiti in Sydney's Central railway station. Packer and Turnbull thought that the leaks from within the commission were systemic, and calculated to harm Packer himself.

"Tackling Costigan by conventional means was futile and I persuaded Packer to counter-attack with a violent public attack on Costigan," is how Turnbull described his tactics four years later. Twenty-four years later, driving between Launceston and Hobart and breaking off periodically to point out striking examples of Georgian architecture, he takes up the story.

"We had a meeting in Kerry Packer's boardroom," he recalls. "Kerry Packer, Jock Harper, Alec Shand and Tom Hughes. We went through what we were going to do and I was very strongly of the view that he needed to counter-attack."

Turnbull, ever eager, had already written an 8000-word press release in which Packer identified himself as the Goanna and savagely refuted the shadowy allegations against him and denounced those who spread them.

"The older gents took a more conservative point of view," Turnbull remembers.

"Kerry, having listened to everyone, said: 'How long do I get for contempt?' Someone said they thought it was five years. 'Then I'll serve that concurrently with the life sentence for murder,' he said.

"There was an old lady called Enid, she ran the Telex in the lobby. She typed off this long statement onto a tape, fed the tape in, and the Telex coughed and spluttered. We looked at it going out, and he said: 'Oh well, the die is cast.'"

Turnbull wasn't even thirty years old. In the following days, he redoubled his efforts, appearing on television and radio on Packer's behalf. His barrister colleagues were horrified at this departure from the doughty orthodoxies of the Bar; Turnbull was no longer functioning as a legal advocate, they thought, but rather as a vastly over-educated bouncer for Packer.

So Turnbull became a solicitor instead, and further scandalised his brethren by continuing his advocacy work under those auspices.

This story alone – like many of the pulsing narratives in which Malcolm Turnbull has been involved as a principal player – would fill its own book. If I race through it here, it is purely for reasons of space.

But it is worth noting that even the opening attack against Costigan did not constitute the high-water mark of Packer and Turnbull's aggression in the case. Packer – represented by Turnbull – commenced defamation proceedings personally against Douglas Meagher QC, who was counsel assisting Costigan.

Turnbull claimed that Meagher had himself leaked the case summaries to the *National Times* via its editor, Brian Toohey. Typically, Turnbull ramped up the legal action with a series of provocative claims in the press, including an interview in which he claimed to have "significant evidence" that Meagher had leaked the documents. That evidence was never adduced: Turnbull and Packer dropped their action, and Meagher's riposte was to have the whole thing struck out as an abuse of process. Justice Hunt, finding for Meagher, delivered a crushing condemnation of Turnbull's style, saying that his statements to the media had "managed effectively to poison the fountain of justice immediately before the commencement of the present proceedings."

Today, Turnbull is finally prepared to spell out the nature of the "incontrovertible, rolled-gold evidence" that he was loath to reveal all those years ago. The smoking gun, he says, was surveillance evidence of a rendezvous between the key players.

"There was a meeting at the Jade Lotus restaurant in Bank Place between Meagher, [journalist] Wendy Bacon and Brian Toohey," he says.

This surveillance evidence, which according to Turnbull was gleaned from an Australian Federal Police officer, was never disclosed to the court.

"We got ourselves into the position where in order to stop Hunt striking the action out we would have had to disclose the basis of our assertion" – something, he says, that would have compromised his informant, who at the time was still employed by the AFP. "There was a lot of anger among people in the law-enforcement agencies about Costigan and Meagher," Turnbull explains.

Toohey says: "I can state categorically that Malcolm Turnbull cannot possibly have any evidence that Douglas Meagher leaked those summaries to me, because he didn't."

From the Costigan affair we can draw some preliminary conclusions about the young Turnbull. The first is that he had no regard for orthodoxy, whether it be the polite (and substantially fictitious, it must be said) convention that barristers do not speak to the press, or the generally accepted view that one should exercise caution when one's client is accused of murder and drug running in what is effectively a closed court.

This refusal to "play by the rules" is something of a lifelong pattern for Turnbull; it explains much of his success, but it also accounts for the worst of his reputation. Breaking the rules, like standing up in the theatre to get a better view, only really works if no-one else is doing it. And breaking the rules, like standing up in the theatre, always causes hard feelings.

Turnbull's aggressive use of the media during the Costigan affair was felt as an affront by legal contemporaries who thought it wasn't quite cricket. His fly-in, fly-out approach to university study caused resentment among fellow students who felt that if they could be bothered to show up to lectures, so should he. And in the NSW state parliamentary press gallery, where Turnbull moonlighted as a radio, TV and print reporter whenever his busy schedule permitted, hard feelings soon developed with some colleagues. Back then, accredited press-gallery reporters had their own dining room, where long lunches would be taken, wine imbibed and war stories exchanged. There were conventions about this stuff; stories heard over lunch were off-limits.

But sometimes, to the other reporters' annoyance, these stories would bob up under Turnbull's by-line in the Nation Review. Hostilities built, and one day when Turnbull made a snide remark to the Channel Ten reporter Paul Mullins about one of his stories, Mullins responded by punching Turnbull to the ground. Mullins, who went on to become a Macquarie Street institution, is now on good terms with Turnbull and declines to discuss the episode, of which he is not proud. But colleagues of the time are in no doubt about what caused the friction.

The second thing we learn from Costigan is that violent tactical methods are not just something to which Turnbull will contemplate turning if sufficiently provoked. It's not enough to say that Turnbull is prepared to play hard-ball. He prefers to play hard-ball – that's the point. It is impossible to rid oneself entirely of the suspicion that Turnbull enjoys the intrigue – the hurling of grenades, the hot denials of drug smuggling, the gathering of surveillance detail on prominent QCs and newspaper editors. Is it any surprise that within two years Turnbull was off on a spy adventure?

Boy's Own Adventure: Spycatcher

When Turnbull set up his own legal practice in 1986 with his friend Bruce McWilliam, one of the first pieces of business he received was a mysterious brief from the barrister Geoffrey Robertson; the mission was to fight for the right of a broken-down former British intelligence officer, Peter Wright, to publish his memoir in Australia against the trenchant opposition of Her Majesty's British government, then led by Margaret Thatcher.

Turnbull scooted about the country vetting Wright and putting together an argument for the case, which had been declared unwinnable by a series of senior barristers.

Mrs Thatcher's cabinet secretary, Sir Robert Armstrong, was the vessel for the British government's staunch resistance to publication. A snowstorm of correspondence and demands for document discovery ensued, as Turnbull – assisted by Lucy – assiduously read everything he could about the spying game. Turnbull remained square-jawed in the face of the thrilling news that his phone was likely to be bugged.

He and his British colleague David Hooper, a lanky toff and old Etonian, devised complex techniques to unnerve the intelligence agencies and Mrs Thatcher's government, particularly Sir Robert Armstrong. They staged elaborately hoaxed discussions to keep the British spooks guessing.

"Is that you, Hoops?" Turnbull would bark down the phone line.

"Absolutely. I have just got back from seeing Boris. He can't get any pictures, or any clear ones."

"How clear are they?"

"Well, I don't think you can be sure it is Armstrong. Boris says it's Armstrong. Apart from the old Etonian tie on the door, there's nothing to indicate it's Armstrong."

"Can you see the mole?"

"No, can't pick that up. I'm just not sure it's Sir Bob. Even though Boris is financing the case, I don't really trust Russians."

And so on. The pair exchanged hoax faxes and delighted in thinking of new ways in which to feed red herrings to their shadowy adversaries.

"The quality of these conversations was not high and generally demonstrated a lamentably ribald lack of respect for our opponents," Turnbull later admitted. "With an eleven-hour time difference between Sydney and London, they generally occurred late either in my night or Hooper's night, and not infrequently after one of us had returned from dinner."

The *Five Go to Spy Island* feel is much enhanced by Turnbull's own account of the affair, which is enclosed within the hardboard covers of his 1988 book, *The Spycatcher Trial*. Halfway through the book, for example – trial underway – Malcolm and Lucy and their chum Paul Greengrass are electrified to discover a cache of secret letters incriminating the British aristocrat Victor Rothschild in the leaking of British intelligence secrets from Wright.

An excitable three-way discussion in the Turnbull home ensues.

"We need to get Peter to cough the lot on Rothschild," decides Turnbull. "We then need to make the allegation about Rothschild public. We need to stir up the Opposition in London with calls to prosecute Rothschild. The government will have to respond by saying they are going to investigate. Rothschild might defend himself by telling the truth."

"If the conspiracy is the truth," corrects Lucy (one senses that she often exercises a moderating role).

"Well, if it isn't, they should bloody well charge him," responds Turnbull hotly. "Anyway, I think we need to get the Labour Party involved ... How do we get onto [the British Labour leader, Neil] Kinnock?"

The vast majority of legal advocates would not think of contacting a politician directly during a trial in an attempt to create helpful political pressure. But our protagonist did not hesitate; within weeks, he had got through to the British Labour leader and given him a brisk set of riding instructions on how to bring down not only Armstrong, but also the British attorney-general, Michael Havers.

The record of the telephone conversation between Kinnock and Turnbull makes for brilliantly weird reading. What other conservative leader in the world is on record as having once rung up and bullied the Labour Party to bring down someone on his own side? And the funniest thing is that Kinnock really did have to be pushed hard, as Turnbull's own account of the conversation illustrates:

> "In order to flush out this lie you have to humiliate Havers. You have to accuse them of legal incompetence, until all of his friends are laughing at him. No matter how mediocre a lawyer he may really be, he is the first law officer and he must have some pride."
>
> Kinnock sounded quite alarmed. "But the real villain is the PM, not Michael. He's sick you know. So's Rothschild for that matter. They are both old men, this business could kill them."
>
> I was quite surprised at this touch of humanity. It was so unlike a politician to be concerned about the health of his opponents. I didn't know what to say, so I made a joke. "Oh well, Comrade, everyone has to make sacrifices for the revolution. Why not start with Havers and Rothschild?" I heard a gasp at the other end.

Kinnock got into trouble just for taking the call from Turnbull; the Australian lawyer was considered something of a public enemy to Britannia at the time. One MP later said that it was as if Kinnock had, during the Falklands War, rung the Argentinian military dictator General Galtieri for a quick chat about tactics.

Turnbull won the case for his client, generating global sales for *Spycatcher* of more than a million copies. To the publisher's great relief, the marketability of the book survived Turnbull's central courtroom defence of it, which was that every disclosure of significance made within the *Spycatcher*'s pages had already been published in existing spy books or in the course of televised interviews. Another victory for Turnbull, who once again had proved himself to be a devastating combination of lawyer, barrister, private investigator, public-relations guru and political strategist.

Adventures in Patricide: Tourang

There are two lessons to be learned about Malcolm Turnbull from his role in the receivership, sale and restructure of the Fairfax media empire in the early 1990s. The first is that Turnbull has limitless determination. The second is that he is virtually unbullyable.

When the sun rose on this new decade, it found Malcolm Turnbull already farcically hyper-involved in the Australian media landscape. To chart his interests properly, you would need a wall-sized sheet of butcher's paper and a good supply of coloured crayons, such was the sinuous interconnection of his various activities.

He was a principal, with Nicholas Whitlam and the former NSW Labor premier Neville Wran, in a merchant bank established with the financial backing of Kerry Packer and the FAI boss Larry Adler. Turnbull has since fallen out with three of those men: Whitlam, and the late Messrs Packer and Adler. One businessman I talked to told me of sitting next to Adler at an insurance-industry lunch, where Adler said of the bank's principals, in his thick Hungarian accent: "Wran is absolutely charming. Whitlam is very lazy, and Malcolm is absolutely crazy."

Here are the highlights of Turnbull's media entanglements from the year 1990. He was a board member at the Nine Network. He advised Westpac on the handling of its $250 million loan to Channel Ten, which made the bank Ten's principal secured creditor. He advised Hudson Conway on its bid for the Seven Network. And he had already taken nearly $10 million in fees from Fairfax, being for extensive advice to the doomed Warwick Fairfax, including a recommendation to sell the *Age* newspaper, which Fairfax ignored.

Viewed at history's clarifying distance, this all looks ridiculous – just too much. But Turnbull at the time was calmly unmoved by allegations that he was too involved.

"All conflicts can be resolved by full disclosure," he told the *Sydney Morning Herald* in 1990. "You say 'Here are all the details, are you happy with it?' And if the client says it's okay, then you're absolved."

To the *Age* he explained that he had a low boredom threshold. "It's all a question of what people need. In order to remain amused, I probably need a high degree of adrenalin and excitement, all that sort of stuff."

Turnbull had an optimistic approach to conflict-of-interest issues even as a young man. In the course of writing his legal column for the *Bulletin* in 1981, for instance, he praised a book called *The Reasonable Men: Trollope's Legal Fiction* for its insights into the British novelist's background in the law.

"It is refreshing, if not surprising, to find someone who maintains that that most pellucid of novelists, Anthony Trollope, owed his literary style to the law," Turnbull wrote approvingly, without mentioning that the author of the work in question, while quite possibly an authoritative voice on Trollope and the law, was also his mother. To call this unorthodox conduct on the part of a reviewer would be understating the matter. But the orthodoxy of disclosure, in this instance, was yet another rule that Turnbull felt he could ignore.

Perhaps we can forgive his filial enthusiasm. After all, what are the odds that your mother will write a book whose subject matter so perfectly lends itself to a mention in your specialised column? He would have found it much harder to disguise a plug for Mum's next book, which was called *The Old Brown Dog: Women, Workers and Vivisection in Edwardian England*.

Not everyone shared Turnbull's sanguine view about managing conflicts of interest between his TV responsibilities, needless to say. In late 1990, Turnbull – working for Westpac – designed a restructure plan for Channel Ten which included a battle plan for dealing with the station's management and its chief executive, Steve Cosser. One of the features of the proposal was Turnbull's idea of circumventing Cosser's expected intransigence by broadcasting Ten's signal, if need be, from the Nine Network's transmitters.

Elements of the plan leaked, creating a widespread belief that Turnbull's management plan involved a low-cost network whose market share would shrink to 10 per cent of the viewing audience. The disclosure of Turnbull's involvement and the leaking of elements of his proposal drew protests from the then communications minister, Kim Beazley, and the chairman of the Trade Practices Commission, Bob Baxt. Baxt issued a warning to Westpac that it should keep Turnbull at arm's length from Ten.

Baxt's letter went out on a Friday. On Sunday, he travelled to Sydney with his wife (the couple lived in Melbourne), to visit his wife's mother. To Baxt's utter astonishment, lunch was interrupted by an angry Malcolm Turnbull, calling the mother-in-law's home phone.

"How did you get this number?" asked Baxt.

"I can get anyone's number if I want to," came Turnbull's chilling reply.

At about this point in the Ten proceedings, Westpac began to develop understandable concerns about the level of political and regulatory fire being drawn by its talented young consultant. With the threat of injunction from the Trade Practices Commission, and the enmity of the federal government, who could blame the bank? Westpac chairman Eric Neal called Turnbull in for a meeting; Turnbull believes that Neal intended to stand him down from the Ten receivership.

"Eric," said Turnbull, with menace. "If you throw me over the gunwale, I will take you by the throat and you will be coming with me. I have done nothing without your authority."

This is the Turnbull from all the stories. The Turnbull who stops at nothing, who threatens and cajoles and heavies his way into what he wants. The man whose indefatigability in pursuit of his objectives does not vary according to the magnitude or importance of the objective; if he wants something, he will do absolutely anything to get it.

"Oh, I don't think any of us have any illusions about Malcolm," says one of his supporters in the Liberal party room, cheerily. "I mean, he would destroy you if you got in his way and think absolutely nothing of it."

The battle for Fairfax is the best demonstration of this. Turnbull, still close to Packer but established in his own merchant bank, watched with interest the deterioration of the Fairfax media company's fortunes as it floundered towards receivership in 1990. There was a profit to be made from the company, once the damage from Warwick's ineptitude had been contained. But how?

Like a dingo prowling the perimeter fence, Turnbull probed here and there for weak points. And found one.

Fairfax was, by late 1990, in serious hock: $1.1 billion to the banks and $450 million to a US-dominated collection of companies holding subordinated debentures; these parties went by the unencouraging title of "junk-bond holders." By late 1990, Fairfax had embarked upon the delicate task of breaking the news to these bond holders that perhaps they and their money should start to make their goodbyes.

But Turnbull offered himself to the junk-bond holders as an advocate, prepared to accept a small salary and expenses on the promise of a healthy success fee should he prevail on their behalf. The Fairfax board, knowing Turnbull's addiction to litigation, was horrified at the prospect of such a partnership: a complicated courtroom fight between Fairfax and its own creditors, the directors reasoned, would decimate confidence in the company and repel buyers.

On Wednesday, 31 October 1990, Fairfax director Bill Beerworth convened a meeting with some of the bond holders in the LA office of their law firm, Coudert Brothers. He was there in the hope of dissuading them from appointing Malcolm Turnbull. But as he spoke, the office door kept opening to admit more of the bond holders, most of whom were far from happy with Fairfax. Harsh words were exchanged. Beerworth began to hand around newspaper clippings about Turnbull – reports of his conflicting media interests and closeness to Packer, of the government's reservations about his role in Channel Ten, and so on.

As this small-scale leafleting took place, the door was once more thrown open and Turnbull himself marched in. He stood for a while enjoying Beerworth's discomfiture, then added his voice to the hostile chorus.

A nasty, uncomfortable scene. But this is a defining characteristic that Turnbull brought to business and the law: he doesn't mind nasty scenes.

And in the end, of course, the prospect of being represented by an aggressive, merciless, cheeky and bargain-priced Australian advocate was more attractive to the junk-bond holders than the prospect of being propelled politely into penury by Fairfax. They signed Turnbull up on the spot. Now the dingo had his chink in the fence.

And he prised it open using his favourite tool: litigation. On behalf of the bond holders, Turnbull commenced legal proceedings within four months against Fairfax and its bankers for misleading and deceptive conduct, claiming that the company had been overly optimistic in its projections when touting for loan funds.

Now, a frenzied exchange of writs-at-ten-paces is not unusual at this level of business. And it was certainly not unusual for Turnbull, who as we know from both the Costigan and the *Spycatcher* episodes regards the court system as an arena for contests of intellect and strategy. But this particular act of litigation imbued Turnbull and the junk-bond holders with a special significance in the great struggle for Fairfax that was about to begin: it gave them a position of relevance.

"Sitting back and watching the banks sell Fairfax and shut out his clients was an option Turnbull was not prepared to entertain," wrote Colleen Ryan and Glenn Burge in their detailed account of the Fairfax affair, *Corporate Cannibals*. "For Turnbull, there is nothing worse than being ignored. If no-one would deal with him, Turnbull had to make sure that he was a force to be reckoned with."

Turnbull, having encouraged his clients to commence the litigation, was the only person who could call it off. Seeing as Fairfax was much more valuable as a going concern than as a ravaged, post-litigation hulk, his ability to make the litigation go away took on a quantifiable market value.

On one construction, this is a stunningly effective legal manoeuvre. On another, it's not entirely unlike the pest exterminator who first releases a bushel of cockroaches into a house, then knocks at the door offering fumigation for a fee. For the Fairfax bankers, the litigation contained an additional and very bitter pill: Turnbull's own firm, working for Fairfax in 1988, had made valuations not dissimilar to those over which Turnbull was now suing.

"Chutzpah is a wonderful Yiddish word, which is best defined as the characteristic of a man who kills both his parents and then throws himself on the mercy of the court on the basis that he is an orphan," wrote Turnbull earlier this year in the *Australian*. Turnbull was applying the word to Kevin Rudd, in recognition of the hide it took for the prime minister to argue in 2007 that he was shoulder to shoulder with John Howard on matters economic, and in 2009 to finger Howard for his destructive adherence to extreme capitalism.

But *chutzpah* is a pretty good term to describe Malcolm's most striking attribute in business, too. *Institutionalised shamelessness* would also come close.

Turnbull's tactics tended to be warmly supported by those on whose behalf they were exercised. Eric Neal, veteran of Turnbull's threats at Westpac, is now Sir Eric, and has done a stint as governor of South Australia.

"He was widely sought-after," recalls the former viceroy admiringly of Turnbull. "His results were always very good."

Kerry Packer, Peter Wright and the American junk-bond holders in Fairfax must certainly have appreciated the wholeheartedness with which Turnbull was prepared to go into battle on their behalf. Here was a man who would cheerfully make enemies among his own peers while serving a client: a rare quality, particularly in the cosy confines of the Australian legal community. There must be great comfort in finding oneself represented by an individual of superior cunning who, moreover, doesn't give a toss if his efforts on your behalf get him invited to fewer golf games. It's only those on the receiving end who moan about breach of convention, or lack of collegiality.

But given Turnbull's rapacious appetite for work, the odds in the '80s and '90s were that if you were involved in media or certain business circles in Sydney, you would probably find yourself pitted against him at some point. Hence the considerable ranks of Malcolm veterans who can't stand him.

"People have always had strong views about me, either positive or negative," he told *Good Weekend* equably in 1988, aged thirty-three. "You don't have to be very successful, contentious or different to be resented in this country. Some people are jealous of almost anybody. You just get on with your life and realise that in terms of business, success doesn't depend on whether people think you're a nice bloke or not."

Well, not when you're in business, maybe.

By dint of ceaseless nagging, coaxing, blustering and persistence, Turnbull parlayed his bond holders' interests into a seat at the table of a most influential bidding consortium, which included Mr Kerry Packer and Mr Conrad Black. Packer, Black and Turnbull met at London's Savoy Hotel on 3 June 1991 to seal the agreement, which included an undertaking from Turnbull's bond holders that they would deal with no other bidders. They called the consortium Tourang.

But the group struggled to prevail, partly due to the public suspicion of Packer's interventionist tendencies as a proprietor, and partly because Tourang did not have quite the rails run it expected in Canberra, where a divisive leadership transition from Hawke to Keating was eroding the influence of the Packer intimate Graham Richardson, of whom much had been hoped. Fairfax journalists rallied against the prospect of Packer's involvement. Word of "The Cat" was whispered around the newsrooms.

"Why do the journos hate me?" Turnbull asked the ABC journalist Quentin Dempster, having invited him in for a cup of coffee and some advice at the height of the journalists' campaign. Dempster had to explain that it was his links to Packer that caused suspicion in many quarters.

Within the Tourang ranks, fissures emerged between some of the gargantuan personalities involved. Trevor Kennedy, the Packer intimate, former rabbit trapper and good friend to Turnbull, was ejected. Packer grew close to a pair of American advisers who told him that Turnbull's continued presence on the Tourang team was a threat to its viability. Turnbull expected a loyal defence from his old boss but – finding none – quickly swallowed his hurt feelings and switched tactics with an extraordinary display of mercurial cunning.

He has never publicly discussed what came next.

It is well known that Packer's presence on the Tourang consortium was skewered sensationally in November 1991 by the leaking of some notes, made by Trevor Kennedy upon his arrival in Tourang, that demonstrated Packer's intentions toward Fairfax to be distinctly more interventionist than his bellicose public avowals gave regulators to believe. Much more recently, it has been reported that Turnbull himself was the shadowy figure who slid into Australian Broadcasting Tribunal chairman Peter Westerway's car one night in a quiet North Sydney street and slipped him a paper bag full of diary notes.

In a car once again, this time driving along Tasmania's Highway One from Launceston to Hobart seventeen years later, Turnbull at last supplies the narrative of that spectacular denouement.

"It was fairly tense," he begins, somewhat superfluously. "I regarded what Kerry was doing as absolutely … it was not only stupid but it was contrary to everyone's interests. And he was taking the view that because he was bigger and richer than me, he could run me into the ground. So I rang Kerry Packer and I had a major row with him. I said, 'If you want to do this, this is it. This is the end. There is no stepping back from this. This is war.'"

Asked about the particulars of his threat to Packer, Turnbull's answer is straightforward: "I told him I'd get him thrown out of the deal. I never make threats I don't carry out." But he has to be pressed quite hard to vouchsafe the exact nature of Packer's response.

"He was fairly upset about it," is the way he puts it at first. Pressed further, he says: "I can't recall." He even lapses briefly into Italian in an attempt to change the subject — "*Avanti, sempre avanti!* (Onward, ever onward)." But eventually, he spells it out.

"Kerry was, um, Kerry got a bit out of control at that time," he says. "He told me he'd kill me, yeah. I didn't think he was completely serious, but I didn't think he was entirely joking either. Look, he could be pretty scary."

Once the disclosure is out, Turnbull warms to the narrative task.

"He did threaten to kill me. And I said to him: 'Well. You'd better make sure that your assassin gets me first because if he misses, you better know I won't miss you.' He could be a complete pig, you know. He could charm the birds out of the trees, but he could be a brute. He could be like that. But the one thing with bullies is that you should never flinch. My father taught me that if someone threatens you with violence, you never, ever succumb. The minute you do, someone will say: 'Oh, so-and-so threatened to belt him and he buckled.'"

Packer, it has been reported, did like to keep a firearm close at hand. The prospect of Australia's richest man flattening himself in a doorway in order to unload a few rounds into Turnbull on his way back from the gym does stretch the imagination somewhat. But there is no doubt that the late Mr Packer was full of surprises. As Turnbull puts it, he was scary.

"He was a difficult, mercurial guy. He could be quite capricious. I had a row with him once, about something he was doing — I can't remember what. I said to him: 'Kerry, this is a very bizarre way to run a business.' He leaned back and said: 'Ah. But what you overlook is that I am a very bizarre person.'"

The die being cast, Turnbull went about his business and delivered the papers to Westerway on the evening of Sunday, 25 November 1991. Westerway, even when told of Turnbull's admission, will not confirm the identity of the man who slipped into the passenger seat of his car just after dusk on a street in Kirribilli, near the Ensemble Theatre, beyond saying that he was a public figure known to him, who had telephoned earlier in the day.

"He rang me and said that he had some material to give me which was of importance or relevance to the inquiry," says Westerway. "He was not prepared to come into the office. So we met on a street down the back of Kirribilli – near a theatre in Kirribilli down the back."

Westerway's source told him, as he handed over the copy of Kennedy's notes, that "he, his wife and family were all at risk."

"He had a genuine apprehension," Westerway recalls of his informant. "Whether it was well-based or not, I have no way of knowing."

On Tuesday, Westerway announced an Australian Broadcasting Tribunal inquiry into Tourang. And on Thursday, Packer withdrew from the consortium. Turnbull only regrets one action at that time: telling Lucy, who was understandably horrified by Packer's threat.

Conrad Black, who remained in the Tourang consortium and went on to win Fairfax without Turnbull or Packer, later wrote of Turnbull that he was "an intelligent, attractive and articulate man, who sometimes has considerable difficulty maintaining his self-control against an onslaught of unimaginable compulsive inner tensions and ineluctable ambitions."

Turnbull and Black spoke after the tumultuous phone call with Packer.

"Black rang me, to try and persuade me [to resign]," Turnbull recalls. "I said, 'Conrad, if you want to be an assassin, you have got to get blood on your hands.'

"He said to me, and I thought it was quite a good answer: 'You don't just want me to have blood on my hands, you want my bloody fingerprints on the dagger.'"

If he feels he is being bullied, Turnbull will respond with full belligerence and no qualms whatsoever. His business career is full of lavish overreactions to threat. Truly, this is a man who would wear a howitzer to a knife fight.

"Well, he started it," is his conclusion on the Packer business. "What do you do? It's like punching somebody and being surprised when they hit you back. I've dealt with a lot of brutes in my time. Jimmy Goldsmith, Conrad Black, [Robert] Maxwell. Rupert, on many occasions. I've dealt with bullies in the corporate world all my life."

There is something of a teenager's braggadocio in Turnbull's defiance of power; something of the paranoiac, too. The language he uses – much talk of "retaliation," "hitting back," "crushing" – is itself laced with aggression. For decades, he has had a crash-bang-wallop approach to conflict, and what appears to be an almost hardwired, violent response to any threat of subordination. He seems perennially to be alert for signs that someone is about to exert their power and influence to dominate him.

"No judge is ever going to run over the top of me. Nobody is going to bully me," he told *Good Weekend* in 1988. "I will not respond to bullying from Mr Cousins, or bullying from any other person who cares to try and bully me," he said in 2007 in response to a campaign by businessman Geoff Cousins against one of Turnbull's decisions as environment minister.

Turnbull's strong public views about bullies do raise a smile in some quarters. For all his identification with journalists, Turnbull is notorious for going over their heads in the event of dispute. When the ABC journalist Sarah Ferguson undertook a profile on Turnbull for the ABC show *Four Corners* in mid-2008, the then shadow treasurer was initially cooperative but developed reservations about the advisability of being seen to promote himself when tensions within the party were so delicately balanced. As negotiations continued, Turnbull emailed the ABC managing director, Mark Scott, to complain about Ferguson.

When Miranda Devine wrote a *Sydney Morning Herald* column critical of Turnbull in 2007, he complained directly to the newspaper's then editor, Alan Oakley. And in a recent speech to a Liberal Forum event hosted by News Limited CEO John Hartigan and attended by several News Limited editors, Turnbull made extensive mention of his closeness to Murdoch. At News, where proximity to the Sun King carries its own privileges, the implicit message to the editors was clear: *Don't mess with me, because I may be able to mess with you.*

Incidentally, one of the stories Turnbull told that night – the tale of how he met Murdoch – is a great example both of Turnbull's *chutzpah* and of the strange way the universe has of occasionally bending to suit him.

Turnbull's overseas holiday in Christmas 1976 was eventful in many ways. He met Harold Evans, as already discussed. He interviewed Enoch Powell. He stayed on and off with Bob Ellis, who was living in Camden. And he received a telegram from Trevor Kennedy, editor of the *Bulletin*, offering him a full-time job. Turnbull was fired by enthusiasm and ambition. He decided to go to New York, where Rupert Murdoch had just bought *New York Magazine* in a hostile takeover, and file a story for Channel Nine about Murdoch's conquest.

Turnbull organised a freelance camera crew and raced about recording interviews. At one point, he was recording a piece to camera next to a newsstand when he noticed the Australian art critic Robert Hughes wandering by. Turnbull collared him and interviewed Hughes on camera; neither man was aware that within five years Turnbull would be married to Hughes's niece, or that a long way down the track Turnbull would convert part of his home into a virtual hospital ward to accommodate the recuperating Hughes after a dreadful car accident. But Turnbull had great trouble getting to Murdoch himself.

"I kept on ringing and ringing and ringing the *New York Post*," says Turnbull. (The *Post* was already owned by Murdoch, and functioned as his New York headquarters.) "He was not giving interviews to anybody. So I just started dialling one extension after another. And finally I fluked it – I got through to the extension on Rupert Murdoch's desk. I said something like 'Jeez, Rupert Murdoch. You've got to help me out. I'm completely screwed!'" Murdoch, presumably impressed by the reporter's persistence, consented to an interview, and Turnbull's bacon was saved.

Just as there's something awe-inspiring about Turnbull's relentless pursuit of Murdoch, there's something spectacular about his defiance of Packer. You have to remember that this is a man barely anyone ever crossed – not this flagrantly, anyway.

Perhaps the most famous footage of Packer is of his quasi-tyrannical appearance before a bank of politicians during parliament's Print Media Inquiry during the Fairfax upheaval. From the moment he introduced himself — "Kerry Francis Bullmore Packer. I appear here reluctantly" — Packer's dominance of the room was apparent, even when viewed through the moderating eye of television. Irascible, wary, reptilian, he wheeled and lunged at his questioners in an unconscious but almost comically perfect vindication of the *National Times'* choice of nickname for him in 1984.

"I think you have a damn hide," Packer snapped at one MP. "I do not intend to cooperate with you in the blackening of my character," he informed another.

Packer was before the inquiry to answer questions about his intentions for Fairfax, but it was a question about his relationship with the Australian Taxation Office that elicited the most memorable quote of the afternoon.

"Of course I minimise my tax," he growled. "Anybody in this country who does not minimise tax wants his head read. I can tell you that as a government you are not spending it so well that we should be donating extra."

Packer was a reclusive character. He existed almost as a fable in this country; a terrifying but elusive miasma of whispered tales in which he ate whole companies alive, or flipped some Texan oilman for $60 million. The rare public appearance before the committee cemented a common view of Packer: here was a man at the peak of his powers, before whom even the parliament quailed, and for whom the payment of tax was a substantially avoidable inconvenience.

Keep in mind, Turnbull's crazy-brave defiance of him took place just seventeen days after that appearance. The Kerry Packer that so dominated a room of politicians of both stripes is the same man that Turnbull set out quite deliberately to goad and destroy.

As is so often the case with Malcolm Turnbull, there is a postscript. Packer and Turnbull, furious with each other, did not speak for two years, although Turnbull spoke to Ros Packer from time to time. Finally, the two men effected a rapprochement: lunch in the back room at Beppi's, a tycoon-infested East Sydney Italian restaurant. The rift finally seemed healed a year before Packer died, when one summer night the ailing mogul and his wife made a rare excursion for dinner down the road to the Turnbulls' place. The two couples sat out on the terrace with a handful of friends until three in the morning, without a trace of rancour; Lucy Turnbull remembers it now as a warm and happy goodbye.

His tactics during the closing phase of the Tourang saga are vintage Turnbull: savage, decisive, and – in a tiny way – childish. There's more than a hint of kicked-over Scrabble board about the whole thing, death threats or no death threats. It's a marvellous story and well told, as any Turnbull story invariably is. The eye goes obediently where it is drawn.

But behind the melodrama, some questions smoulder away insistently. First, there is the small but extremely piquant irony that the man who now says he feared for his life at Packer's hands in 1991 was the same man who, ten years earlier, summoned all his considerable powers of audacity and outrage to defend Packer against the suggestion that he would ever engage in violence. More significantly, there is the question of the Kennedy notes themselves and what they revealed.

The Kennedy notes skewered Packer's involvement in the Fairfax bid because they revealed that Packer had lied to the parliamentary inquiry about the extent of his planned involvement in Fairfax. But Turnbull did not leak the notes to defend the integrity of the parliamentary record, or to strike a blow for freedom of the press.

He leaked them, according to his own graphic account, in order to teach Packer a lesson.

Had Packer not decided to cut his protégé loose, are we to assume that Turnbull would have remained peaceably complicit in the deception? In fairness to Turnbull, the leaking of the documents and the ousting of Packer from the Tourang bid did work in favour of Turnbull's clients, the junk-bond holders. With Packer out of the consortium, Tourang's was a much easier bid for the government to approve, and approve it they did, ensuring the satisfaction of the US creditors.

But this story crystallises something about Turnbull that obsesses his critics, and even bothers some of his supporters in quiet moments. Turnbull is an opportunist – a brilliant, charming, savage gun for hire. A lawyer, when all's said and done, with a considerable gift for argument combined with an unbelievable degree of persistence. His tactical abilities are all the freer for being unrestrained by excessive concern for consistency or even – in some circumstances – governing principle.

This is, unmistakably, a handy quality in business. But in politics, it becomes complicated.

The Tourang affair is the stand-out example, from Turnbull's career in business, of how far Turnbull is prepared to go to prove a point. And echoes of Turnbull's business style do reverberate in his approach to politics.

In the unblinking pursuit of Fairfax, for example, one can easily spot the seeds of Turnbull's hostile takeover of the seat of Wentworth. In both circumstances, he used a combination of lateral thinking, charm, brutality and astute legal manoeuvring to extract results.

In the main, and with the exception of his convictions about tax reform, the values with which Turnbull is identified are soft values – that is to say, they concern enveloping themes rather than hard reforms. Like the duke of the Italian Renaissance, he is a libertarian in the classic sense, for all that these views may co-exist with a savage talent for warfare.

Here we encounter the most significant dissimilarity between John Howard and Malcolm Turnbull. Howard, as a politician, was an unprepossessing physical presence who was fiercely memorable for his convictions and what he did about them. Malcolm Turnbull, on the other hand, is memorable for himself – for the person that he is, for his powerful character traits – more than for his convictions, which are of a much broader inclination than John Howard's specific policy obsessions. Howard may have been a political bird of rather drab plumage personally, but ideologically he was positively eye-catching. His convictions on industrial-relations reform, for example, were at the heart of many of the Liberal Party's terrible internecine battles of the 1980s and early 1990s.

Think of this period as a *West Side Story* of conservative politics; an ideological dance-off between the Dries, headed by the small but perfectly formed industrial hardliner John Howard, and the Wets, whose figurehead more often than not was the urban Melbourne sophisticate Andrew Peacock.

In 1986, the Dries formed a club called the H.R. Nicholls Society, under whose banner they gathered to discuss industrial-relations reform. The Wets countered with a loose grouping that came to be known as The Black Hand. Peter Costello, it should be noted, was a foundation member of the H.R. Nicholls Society and fought very much in John Howard's corner during the bruising policy debates of that era. He was considered an unimpeachable Dry. It was only when the two men's views as to the Liberal leadership succession began to diverge that Costello came to be associated with some damper causes. Now that Howard is gone, Costello has migrated firmly back towards the right wing of the party, and his Wet champions from the Howard era have transferred their allegiance to Turnbull.

That Malcolm Turnbull is wholly unlike John Howard is both his strength and his weakness. No-one else in the party could provide the break from the past and from Howard that Turnbull can. But an institution, to borrow Emerson's lovely line, is the lengthened shadow of one man. And in the modern-day Liberal Party, that man is John Howard.

Howard once described himself, now famously, as "the most conservative leader the Liberal Party has ever had."

George Brandis, who is a Queensland barrister and the shadow attorney-general, has a theory about John Howard. He believes that the Howard era achieved, over time, a precise inversion of Deakin's Liberal Party, which combined liberal social values with a conservative approach to economic policy. Howard, Brandis argues, made the Liberal Party conservative socially and radical economically.

When this theory is put to him, Howard wrinkles his nose. He read Brandis's essay with interest, but does not agree.

"I think that you can strain to hold true to an historical analogy," he says. "Deakin lived and governed before World War I. It's even a stretch to compare many of the circumstances we now face with the circumstances that Menzies faced."

Howard does, however, agree with the assessment that he combined social conservatism with economic adventurism. It was deliberate, he says.

"People want a bit of constancy in their lives. If you've got a lot of rapid economic change, you want a bit of anchorage in ordinary life. The one, in a sense, reinforces and complements the other. The key to our success in office was that we did, generally speaking, govern according to the principles of liberalism in economic policy and with a fairly conservative social agenda which I not only believed in but was also appropriate for the times."

It's a striking thought. And no doubt comforting for lesbians, who might now begin to understand the small part their being banned from IVF treatments might have played in defraying the nation's anxiety about tariff reform.

To the Liberal Party of John Howard, Malcolm Turnbull is like a handsome stranger who turns up on a cruise boat. He's charming, he's witty, he's erudite and he's happy to buy the drinks. So why, oh why, do they hang back?

It can't be a "new money" thing. The Liberal Party does not have the same sensitivity to this as does the British Conservative Party, where it was once disparagingly said of Margaret Thatcher's challenger Michael Heseltine that he "bought his own furniture."

It's more a "new membership" thing. The Liberal Party is like a gentlemen's club, in some respects. Anyone can join, and be treated politely. But after a few years, when you notice you're not getting anywhere, it might occur to you that in some way you are not quite the ticket. To some in the Liberal Party, Malcolm Turnbull is not quite the ticket. Perhaps it is the manner in which he seized the seat of Wentworth. Most definitely it has to do with Turnbull's tin ear for the unwritten codes of the Liberal Party.

"Malcolm doesn't always realise that in the Liberal Party, when somebody raises an eyebrow at you, it actually means something," laughs one Liberal warhorse, a supporter of Turnbull.

As a result, Turnbull often commits howlers, such as the time he was addressing his colleagues and pointed out to them the curious habit Kevin Rudd has of mentioning him – Turnbull – all the time. "Neville Wran, whom I regard as a great political strategist, told me he made it a practice never to mention his opponents by name," Turnbull informed the meeting. Or the time – again at a party meeting – when he mused aloud on his suspicion that the former Labor prime minister Paul Keating was coaching Rudd and Swan behind the scenes. "I rang Keating, and I said to him: 'You're helping them, aren't you?'" Turnbull told his flock.

Now, in front of any other crowd, neither of these remarks would seem exceptional, let alone exceptionable. But Liberal MPs are a sensitive lot, and the effect was rather like a meeting of Orangemen hearing their preacher make a breezy reference to having phoned the Pope the other day.

Turnbull is candid by inclination, and when he was asked in May 2008 about the controversy surrounding the new photographic works of Bill Henson, he gave an instinctive libertarian reply.

"I think we have a culture of great artistic freedom in this country and I don't believe the vice squad's role is to go into art galleries," he said. Turnbull was the only politician in Australia who voiced any support for Henson during the national outbreak of moralistic fervour that accompanied that artist's fateful exhibition, which was staged at the Roslyn Oxley Gallery, in Turnbull's electorate.

Turnbull's comments whizzed around the parliamentary Liberal Party, many of whose members felt that they demonstrated a chronic lack of judgment. All very well to support artists, it was felt, but not in public – not when sentiment against Henson's work was running so high. Brendan Nelson declared, on behalf of the Liberals, that Henson's images of naked children "violated Australian values." After he made those remarks, Nelson received a call from Malcolm Turnbull, who berated him: "Do you know how many art galleries I have in my electorate?"

Turnbull's instincts are often at odds with the received wisdom inside the party he leads.

"Malcolm Turnbull will destroy the Liberal Party," Peter Costello told one backbencher I spoke to. And I wish I had ten bucks for every time someone said to me, in the course of researching this essay, "Malcolm is not a creature of the Liberal Party." To be fair to him and them, not everybody meant that remark as a criticism.

But the ones that did meant that it is not possible to lead an organisation that you don't understand. And Turnbull, for all that he is a quick learner, only rejoined the Liberal Party in 2000, and only arrived in Parliament in 2004 at age fifty. History whispers that late arrival is a disadvantage; apart from Bob Hawke, the prime ministers of recent decades tend to have entered parliament early: Malcolm Fraser at twenty-five, Paul Keating at twenty-five, John Howard at thirty-four, Gough Whitlam at thirty-six.

Peter Costello entered parliament at age thirty.

Alexander Downer, who is definitely a creature of the Liberal Party, is quick to defend Turnbull from critics who believe his lack of flight-hours in the Liberal Party prevents him from leading it effectively.

"It's sort of patronising, that view. I mean, what is the argument here? That he can't learn? Sure, he came into the Liberal Party and into power not knowing as much as people who had been there for twenty years, like me or John Howard or Peter Costello. But people aren't actually born to understand the Liberal Party. You have to learn."

Michael Kroger, whose authority within the Liberal Party is undimmed by his failure to go into parliament, is also very much a creature of the party. His support for Malcolm Turnbull is complicated slightly by the fact that he is Peter Costello's best friend.

"He's always been inside the tent," Kroger insists of Turnbull. "Partly because of Tom Hughes, and his close association with Tom Hughes for family reasons, he's always been around the party. He's got a much deeper association with the Liberal Party than Brendan Nelson, who was a member of the ALP for many years."

Yet Turnbull does have an unusually broadminded approach to friendship with Labor figures. Of the four former Labor premiers of NSW still alive, Turnbull has had close friendships with two: Neville Wran and Bob Carr. Let's not forget his fascination with Lang. And his work for the WA Labor government of Peter Dowding co-existed with a warm personal friendship with Dowding himself; after Dowding lost the premiership, he moved into one of Turnbull's spare houses in Sydney as a tenant.

To befriend one Labor premier might, for someone who is now the leader of the Liberal Party, be viewed as excusable. To befriend two is bordering on careless. But four? It begins to look like a pattern. And it is one of the reasons why elements within the Liberal Party really aren't quite sure about their current federal leader.

Let's not muck about: what's the view of the Liberal Party's most significant living creature on all of this?

John Howard considers the question. "There's a bit of a crossover in Sydney," he says, eventually. "Socially, a lot of Labor and Liberal people will see each other. Particularly in the eastern suburbs."

The former prime minister enunciates these words with studied neutrality. He is right, up to a point, and it's a heroic effort on the part of Howard, in whom one senses an amused (if faintly consternated) indulgence of Turnbull. But in order to test the orthodoxy of this view within the Liberal Party, one needs only attempt to picture John Howard himself, out on the tiles with a rainbow crowd of artists, eastern suburbs property developers and Labor grandees. See what I mean?

Rallying, Howard makes the point that there are "no iron rules" about this sort of thing.

"I mean, has Kevin Rudd really been entrenched in the Labor Party? Was Rudd really active in the Labor movement the way that Keating was?" Howard has a point here; if it is said of Malcolm Turnbull that he could in another life have been a Labor leader, it could equally be said of Kevin Rudd that he would not look out of place in the Liberal Party.

Politics in Australia presently has about it a sense of exhaustion. For all Kevin Rudd's essayism, it is hard to place him in the Labor pantheon. Of all the Coalition policies that caused Labor heartburn on the Opposition benches – Work Choices, Iraq, the mandatory detention of asylum seekers, the 30 per cent private health insurance rebate, increases to university fees, increased funding to private schools, the privatisation of Telstra and the employment-services network, the Northern Territory intervention, and many more – only Iraq and Work Choices have been largely reversed by Kevin Rudd, with the May Budget delivering more of a Labor-style haircut than a full makeover.

And of all the grand arguments that have gone into industrial relations over the years, all the rioting and division and heartache and sheer difficulty, the main point over which Labor and Liberal were left haggling when the Rudd government's bills hit the Senate was this: should a small business be defined as a business with twenty employees or fifteen?

"These debates to a large extent have been won by the conservatives," argues Michel Kroger. "All of the industrial-relations debates were basically won by Howard. Family policies, deregulation, privatisation, surplus budgeting, efficiencies in the public service – all won by the conservatives. Twenty years ago the debates were about the centralised wage system. Or about enterprise-bargaining disputes between the federal and state commissions. Contractors, employees and compulsory unionism. The argument on these things is now going on at the fringes.

"Don't forget," warns Kroger, "that as the ideological divide has narrowed, the place of ideologues has become less important. Many who joined the party who were deeply rooted in anti-communist beliefs – well, now there's very few joining the party because of that. Politics is less ideological than it was, therefore you're not going to get as many people driven by the ideology as there was in days gone by."

Of the differences between Kevin Rudd and Malcolm Turnbull, the largest is a matter of tendency rather than brute ideology. Rudd tends to be a fiddler; Turnbull tends toward non-intervention.

"I am not an ideological person," he told Fran Kelly late last year. "I am a practical person. I come with a long experience in business. My interest is in things that work, in things that deliver real results for people that are relevant. I'm not interested in ideological wars. I'm interested in getting real results for the people of Australia and I'm very – I am very, very well aware, Fran, of how Australians think."

When I first go to see Malcolm Turnbull about writing this essay, he is already settled in suite RG109 in Parliament's House of Representatives wing – the office of the Opposition leader. It's quite a pleasant suite; its corner office, earmarked for the Opposition leader's chief of staff, commands a good view of the courtyard through which MPs and ministers often pass on their way to Question Time.

But it's not an office that's hosted much by way of happy times over the course of its recent history. Of RG109's five previous occupants – Brendan Nelson, Kevin Rudd, Simon Crean, Mark Latham and Kim Beazley – only one has achieved the common goal of quitting it for the office thirty metres to the north.

The place looks different from when Brendan Nelson worked here. A big William Robinson painting hangs on the wall opposite the door, for example. It's a good one, a huge canvas from Robinson's endearing barnyard series, on which two dozen lovely chooks strut this way and that, eyes bright and quizzical and combs comically awry. It doesn't belong to the Parliament House art collection. It belongs to the Turnbulls, and it must be a quarter of a million dollars' worth of painting, at the very least. Lucy bought it originally for their farm, because the farm manager disapproved of chickens and Lucy felt that a farm without chickens was incomplete. Now that the painting has been relocated to Canberra, it provides comic relief to the principal occupant of suite RG109.

"Alex [Downer] and I used to amuse ourselves by working out which chooks reminded us of which colleagues," remarks Turnbull, when I admire the painting. "Alex always wanted to be that one there" – indicating a splendid rooster.

Downer and Turnbull are much better friends than is widely recognised. As foreign affairs minister, Downer used regularly to stay at the Point Piper house, enjoying the hospitality of the Turnbulls' home with its good cellar and gorgeous views.

"Well, I have known him since we both stood in preselections in 1981," says Downer. "I stood for the preselection in Boothby, and he stood for Wentworth. We both lost, and we commiserated with each other on the grounds that it was perfectly obvious that the worst candidates had won. We agreed that we were the stand-out talent, and the tragedy for the nation was that it would now have to wait for that which could quite easily have been its at an earlier date."

Talking to Downer is always fun. He is much more amusing than it might appear from his press conferences or television appearances – funny in a raucous and faintly inappropriate way. One senses that he is always teetering on the edge of a blithe solecism of one kind or another.

The drawback of being a journalist in conversation with Downer is that one must gird oneself at every turn for his jibes at journalists, every man jack of whom he firmly believes to be a devoted agent of the Australian Labor Party. Thus, he peppers his monologues with commentary. Halfway through an attack on Rudd's Monthly essay, he interrupts himself contentedly – "Journalists will never report this, of course, because they love all that socialist stuff."

I remember once having a drink with Downer at his hotel in London; he was in terrific form, regally sharing the drinks trolley in his suite at the Berkeley and puffing on his pipe. Is it my imagination, or is it possible that he was wearing a smoking jacket? "Yes, but you would say that," I remember him declaring grandly at one point, waving his pipe in response to a perfectly ordinary point I'd made – "You're Labor." After a while, one becomes accustomed to it. Interviewing Downer, one feels a little like an old-style typewriter. There's a line of useable copy, then there's a vigorous slap, and then another line of copy, and then another slap, and that's the way it goes, and you can't get the copy unless you're prepared to put up with the slaps.

There are a couple of reasons why you wouldn't expect Downer to be a big supporter of Malcolm Turnbull's. First, Downer is a creature of the Liberal Party in a way Turnbull could never be; in pedigree terms, he plays a regal poodle to Turnbull's talented bitzer. Secondly, Downer's best friend in politics is his fellow South Australian, the Coalition's Senate leader Nick Minchin.

Both Downer and Minchin threw themselves with great energy into defeating Turnbull's "Yes" campaign for the republic referendum in 1999. But when, in November 2007, the Liberal Party found itself confronted with a choice between Brendan Nelson and Malcolm Turnbull, only Minchin settled back into the old slot of opposition to Turnbull.

Downer backed Turnbull, and voted accordingly. How did Downer and Turnbull become friends? There's no deep, Machiavellian conspiracy here, or blood pact to take over the Liberal Party. The two men just like each other; they make each other laugh.

"Malcolm's self-confident enough to be relaxed about being friendly with people who disagree with him," says Downer, adding airily: "He has heaps of enemies, but I suppose they are born out of jealousy and defeat."

Turnbull's entrée to the seat of Wentworth was not without bloodshed.

No, that's a drab way of putting it; let's say that in order to contest the seat for the Liberal Party, Turnbull had first to remove a stubborn sitting member, Peter King, in circumstances of – for the Liberal Party – sickening political violence. In the course of this process, an estimated 1500 new members were signed up to Turnbull's home branch of Point Piper. Cynics call this "branch-stacking." Euphemists call it "growing democracy."

The King forces stacked back just as fast as they could, and Turnbull countered with complicated legal challenges to the official status of their stackees.

King fought determinedly, but in the end was utterly outclassed.

"When he came up against Turnbull, he came up against a speeding train," muses Downer. John Howard, who has in the past intervened to protect sitting members from this sort of attack, sat on his hands.

"I think I can put it this way," the former prime minister smiles broadly, when asked if he supported Turnbull's bid. "I didn't stop him getting preselection for Wentworth. He was prepared to have a go and I quite respected that. I didn't have anything against Peter King, but on the other hand Peter had knocked off the previous sitting member and I didn't think he could cry foul against Malcolm."

Before nominating for Wentworth, Turnbull sent a careful inquiry via the former party director Lynton Crosby to ascertain whether Howard would object to his candidacy. No such objection was expressed.

There was, of course, the business of Turnbull's verbal attack on Howard at the end of his unsuccessful campaign for an Australian republic, in which he called Howard "the prime minister who broke the nation's heart."

"Oh, I didn't care about that," says Howard, with a dismissive fly-swat motion of his hand.

Alexander Downer corroborates this. "There's a press-gallery theory," he begins (slap!) "that Howard hated or resented Turnbull for his comment that the PM had broken the nation's heart. But John Howard saw that comment for what it was. He just laughed. It was an amusing and inappropriate comment."

Turnbull's takeover of Wentworth had all the sweep and grandeur of a Labor branch-stack. When he arrived in Canberra, it was to a Coalition scandalised by the scale of the violence: it was as if a genteel bridge party had now to contend with a barbarian wearing the freshly flayed skin of the deputy secretary for scones.

Nor did much of the new environment naturally accord with Malcolm the Barbarian. He was flummoxed to learn that he would have to fill out, by hand, a declaration of all his assets and interests.

The Register of Members' Interests is a pleasantly anachronistic ritual, breach of which is nonetheless a catastrophic error. New and returning MPs are issued with photocopied forms, with spaces for things such as "real property" and "commercial investments." By picking up a completed set of forms and weighing it in one's hand, eyes closed, one can make a fair guess as to the political allegiance of the author. Labor MPs have, on the whole, shorter declarations, although earnest left-wingers wishing to make much of their modest circumstances will occasionally stray in the other direction by declaring everything from their Westpac Handycard account to the two bucks they gave to the Salvation Army collector on 15 January.

Liberal and National Party MPs are much more likely to have complicated share holdings, and family trusts called "Macbarhel" or "Sartombri" or some other clunky agglomerate of their children's names.

Malcolm Turnbull's declaration, however, is seriously weighty. In his most recent return, made upon his re-election to parliament in 2007, Turnbull declared shareholdings in four listed companies, five unlisted public companies, eight private companies and twenty-five managed funds.

At the very end of the form is a space in which MPs are asked if there is anything at all remaining to declare; any asset worth more than $7500 after all the other categories have been covered. Most MPs have by now exhausted their worldly goods, but Turnbull has enough left for a brutally affluent final volley: "Boats, Artwork, Books, Furniture."

The Turnbulls own a waterfront apartment in Canberra, which nests high on one of the city's new developments that crowd round the southern shores of Lake Burley Griffin. The apartment is in Lucy Turnbull's name, and her husband – consistent with his parliamentary travel-allowance entitlements – pays her around $180 a night in rent when he is in town. Over his years in Canberra, Turnbull has frequently hosted groups of colleagues at his Canberra digs for informal evenings with takeaway food and conversation.

His accommodation is a notch higher than it could have been. Joe Hockey owns a house in Manuka, not far from Parliament House in the middle of Canberra's café district. He has played genial landlord to a succession of colleagues over the years, including the former Victorian Liberal MP Phil Barresi, the shadow defence minister Bob Baldwin, and the former Liberal leader Brendan Nelson. (Nelson, who cultivates a reputation for asceticism, lives in the garage and cheerfully eschews heating.)

When Turnbull arrived in Canberra after the 2004 election, Hockey – always on the lookout for fun housemates – tried to interest him in the spare room. Turnbull, who had no intention whatsoever of moving in, nevertheless politely agreed to go and inspect the premises. When he arrived early one morning, it was in time to witness a near-naked Baldwin (one of parliament's larger gents) wandering down the hall and into the bathroom for a noisy visit.

"He seemed to be wearing a hand-towel. Or it looked like a hand-towel," a scarred Turnbull recalled. Turnbull fled on the barest of excuses, and Lucy soon bought her investment property.

The gory dispatching of Peter King gave Turnbull senior ogre status in the parliamentary Liberal Party before he even got there.

"Some of them loathed him because of it," Downer says. "There's this sort of idea that particularly less-worthy backbenchers have that there is sort of a pecking order. They thought he was a *parvenu*."

The *Oxford English Dictionary* defines a *parvenu* as "A person from a humble background who has rapidly gained wealth or an influential social position; a *nouveau riche*; an upstart, a social climber."

"There was a bit of jealousy and bitterness about him," concludes Downer. "My advice to him was 'just go quietly, and you'll rise.'"

Another who offered Turnbull advice during this period, oddly enough given what was to come, was Brendan Nelson. Nelson says he approached Turnbull in the poky backbencher's office to which the former merchant banker was initially assigned.

"I said to him: 'Look – I don't ever forget being elected myself. You've achieved a lot in your life – far more than I have in mine. Sometimes you'll look at someone who is a minister and you'll think, 'Why is he a minister when I'm a backbencher? I'm much smarter than him.' But the important thing is to realise that none of us is any better or any worse than anybody else. There are people I work with here that I don't like. But they'll never know that I don't like them. You've got to rise from obscurity.'"

Nelson's little homily was sincere; he was impressed by Turnbull's accomplishments, and genuinely concerned as to what Turnbull would make of his new surroundings, littered as they were with people who were considerably stupider than Turnbull, but considerably senior to him.

It is difficult to overstate the significance of what happened to the Liberal Party in late November 2007.

It lost government, of course. It lost its leader, too, in an outcome that was probably kindest for him; voted out of his own seat, John Howard was not obliged to choose between shrivelling away publicly on the back-benches or submitting the innocent people of Bennelong to a by-election.

But then it lost its Plan B, too. Peter Costello, to the amazement of nearly everyone, decided not to lead the Liberals after all. At a press conference on the Sunday after the election, he announced that he would be leaving politics in due course to embark upon a career in the corporate world.

"He spoke to me the night before," remembers Howard. "He indicated to me that he was in some doubt." But Costello had mused aloud to Howard before on his uncertainty about the future. "He'd occasionally say 'I don't know what to do.' 'There's no money in this.'"

Howard always thought Costello would stick around. "I thought to myself, well, politics is in his blood like it is in mine. And how could you ever give up one of the safest seats in the country?"

When Costello announced he would depart rather than take up the leadership, it was as though the backbone had been removed from the Liberal Party. Stripped of the two men who had given it form and sub-stance for thirteen years, this luckless invertebrate flopped about in search of a new leader.

"I was flabbergasted," remembers Brendan Nelson of that day. "I was on the phone to Joe Hockey, having decided to run for deputy when I got the news that Peter wasn't going to run. Then I thought, from his perspec-tive, I could completely understand why he wouldn't. He'd been incred-ibly close to the prime ministership and the leadership of the party and that hadn't happened. The fact is that whoever leads after an election defeat like that is almost certainly not going to be the next prime minister – immediately at least."

Malcolm Turnbull was quick to step up. So quick, in fact, that there are a couple of MPs and senators who reckon they only became aware of Peter Costello's withdrawal when Turnbull called them seeking their support. Nelson, after a lot of thought, decided to run too.

"I knew it was going to be hard, it was going to be thankless. I knew all that. But I believe in life you've got to have a go. I had a lot of support. And I'd seen a bit of Malcolm in the twelve months he'd been in cabinet. Enough to motivate me to see that there would be a contest."

There was a strange, light-headed feel about the short campaign that ensued before Coalition MPs and senators gathered in Canberra to make the choice between Nelson and Turnbull. For many, it was like one of those childhood dreams in which all the roles are played by the wrong people; where you turn up to school and you notice that you're not at school at all, but at the Easter Show, and your teacher's turned into Daryl Somers, and you're wearing a snorkel.

"The problem with that ballot is that nobody saw it coming," says Howard. "Nobody expected there to be a ballot between Brendan Nelson and Malcolm Turnbull."

Turnbull was convinced, with Costello out of the way, that he was the obvious choice. On the day before the leadership ballot, Turnbull gave an interview to Fran Kelly, of the ABC's Radio National. It was a confident performance; too confident for some.

Kelly: In the past, sometimes John Howard's leadership was described as mean and tricky. Would you describe yours, if you were Liberal leader, as more generous?

Turnbull: Very much so.

Kelly: Should Work Choices be dumped?

Turnbull: Look, there is no question that Kevin Rudd has a mandate to make changes to Work Choices.

Kelly: Would you support Labor in saying "Sorry" to the stolen generations?

Turnbull: Unquestionably. That was, look, that was an error. I say this about, you know, a friend, John Howard: that was an error. Clearly, we should have said sorry then.

The above is an edited selection of Turnbull's remarks.

There was plenty about the interview that grated with Liberals who knew there had to be some renovations, but weren't quite prepared for the sight of Turnbull with his raised sledgehammer. To Turnbull's great surprise, Brendan Nelson won the ballot, with forty-five votes to forty-two.

"That was a silly interview," is Howard's assessment of Turnbull's campaign style. "He probably did think he was going to win, and that damaged him. The issue that he floated in that interview – the apology – is an example of the danger that politicians get into. The apology had a huge run and everybody says Rudd did a good job with it … but it didn't shift a vote."

The former PM has moved seamlessly into metapolitics here. He's not making a point about the merits of a national apology, in the argument over which his own position in government ended up hopelessly ensnarled in a brain-numbing semiotic debate about the difference between regret and remorse. He's making a point about the political smarts of Malcolm Turnbull for even raising it. (As for the apology itself: "I demonstrated my position by not attending. It would have been hypocritical for me to go.")

Nelson was overcome with emotion and humility upon his election to the leadership. Like a long-shot actor finding himself on stage grasping an Oscar, Nelson gave a teary speech in which he thanked Malcolm Turnbull, John Howard, Peter Costello, Mark Vaile and Alexander Downer, before solemnly warning his remaining colleagues that they faced a long and difficult road ahead.

Turnbull couldn't quite believe he had lost. "It was like the captain of the football team, who was also the rowing blue and the captain of the debating team and dux of the school, watching as the headmaster chooses someone else to be head boy," recalls one colleague. And he was disgusted by Nelson's weepy display. After the meeting but before Nelson's first press conference, Turnbull barrelled into Nelson's office, startling the small group that was already in there with the new leader.

"Brendan, that was terrible. It was funereal!" he stormed, waving his arms in the full Turnbull display. "Come on! You have to gee them up, like a football coach. Not depress them!"

Several weeks later, when Nelson was out in the car, Turnbull rang him again. "Let's face it, Brendan," he said. "You're just no good at this. The best thing you could do is just step down."

Recalling the intervention in Nelson's office, Turnbull grimaces. "I was trying to help him!" he protests.

It sounds disingenuous, but Turnbull is serious. Turnbull is a creature of conflict. As he says, he has dealt with a lot of brutes. He is steeped in conflict, and as a result somewhat inured to it, and often fails to notice when he has given offence. Or sincerely cannot understand why people feel affronted by his manner. This is one of Malcolm Turnbull's key character attributes, and a source of much confusion, one suspects.

In Turnbull's view, it was absolutely plain that Nelson was going to be a disaster. It was equally plain, in Turnbull's mind, that Turnbull would do a considerably better job. Giving Nelson tips on how to address their colleagues was, on that basis, a kindness rather than an assault.

Turnbull has also tried to "help" Kevin Rudd, on occasion. The two men often run into each other at major events. Over the years, each has listened to the other speak many times, and at Jewish events Turnbull has several times fretted privately over Rudd's pronunciation of Yiddish terms.

Recently, at one such occasion, Turnbull pulled the prime minister aside just before he was due to speak.

"Listen, Kevin. It's not in my interests to help you, but you should know that Yiddish words with a 'ch' aren't pronounced like the 'ch' in 'cherry.' It's more like this." Here Turnbull produced a throaty hawking sound, as if preparing to spit, while Rudd stared at him coldly. "For example 'Chanukah' is pronounced 'Hhhhhanukah.' Just letting you know. Really, it's worth getting it right."

You can imagine how thrilled Rudd was to receive this tutorial.

The Rudd–Turnbull match-up is rich in comedy, largely due to their unconscious similarities. Each of them is privately, independently and unshakeably convinced of his utter superiority over the other, and there are very few things in life that are funnier than watching two such people interact.

Both of them grew up in reasonably straitened circumstances, and both of them are now wealthy thanks to hard work and a flair for business – in Rudd's case, the flair is largely that of his wife, Therese Rein.

Both converted for their wives: Turnbull made the leap to Catholicism, while Rudd made the much rarer transition in the opposite direction. Both men are intellectually strong, and both prefer their own counsel to that of others. Neither man is easy to work for.

Turnbull's advantage over Rudd is that he is much more comfortable in the world of private enterprise, and is a far better speaker and can communicate without resort to the use of jargon. Rudd's advantage over Turnbull is that he is much more comfortable in the world of the bureaucracy, and understands that the building of a political narrative has much to do with the senseless repetition of drab phrases.

Rudd's contempt for Turnbull is apparent in parliament, where he regularly discusses and disparages the Liberal leader, whom he calls the "Member for Goldman Sachs." Turnbull, who often tries to engage Rudd in pleasant banter over the dispatch box and is usually rebuffed, puzzled over the PM's unfriendliness in an interview with the *Courier Mail* in late 2008.

"For someone who trained as a diplomat, he is often very undiplomatic," Turnbull mused. "He is very chilly towards me. He is odd."

With Brendan Nelson, Turnbull's criticisms sprang from a simple conviction that Nelson was a terrible leader and would never get anywhere – an opinion with a solid basis in the published polls that seemed, every month, to get worse and worse. The irony, of course, is that under Nelson the party did everything that Turnbull so alarmed them by promising it would do under him: agreed to the ratification of the Kyoto Protocol, signed up to the national apology, retreated from Work Choices.

Oddly enough, Nelson's victory in that first ballot turned out to be the best thing that could have happened to Turnbull. Nelson soothed the party through some of its necessary transformations and functioned as a sort of human shock absorber.

There are many pitfalls in becoming the leader of a party that has just been flung out after a long period in government. It's not just that such leaders are almost certain, statistically, never to become prime minister. It's also that when ordinary MPs land on the Opposition benches after years of rigorous discipline in government, many view it as a chance to let off steam.

"I've bitten my tongue for ten years and what good's it done me?" is how the thinking typically goes. Already faced with the ignominy of a poky office, fewer staff and a smaller pay packet, therefore, the brand-new leader of the Opposition also has to be prepared to work sensitively with Backbencher X, who feels that life won't be worth living again until he's delivered a four-hour parliamentary attack on the single-desk wheat-export policy.

Nelson was actually pretty good at this part of the job.

One of his most irksome qualities as a political leader was a Gothic fascination with human suffering that rendered him unable to complete a formal speech without reference to suicide rates, child rape or gestational diabetes. (Nelson gets to about the ninety-minute mark of our interview before mentioning suicide, which must be a personal best.) In the way that hypochondriacs can be spectacularly good with sick people, Nelson showed a deft hand with the traumatised souls within his party, recognising their need just to be heard for a while.

On the question of the national apology, he argued publicly both for and against it. At the time, it sounded as though Nelson was arguing with himself, and not always winning either. Nelson explains that his primary audience during this process was his colleagues, not the general public.

"My own view was that politically and morally we had to apologise," he says. "But I knew it would involve having to use myself to get them there. So they would say, 'He gets it. He understands how we feel.' You couldn't, under the circumstances we'd been through, just say as the leader, 'We will support the apology.'"

Nelson saw himself as a sort of political midwife, soothing and minimising the birthing difficulties associated with a new policy approach. Leadership by group therapy might be another way to put it.

John Howard, one year and four months after losing his prime minister-ship and his seat, is in rude good health.

His new office, located on the 53rd floor of Sydney's MLC building, com-mands a sparkling view of the harbour. His staff bustle about amid a dis-ordered scene; literally hundreds of framed photographs and mementos lie stacked against walls, or piled four and five deep on the furniture in the reception area. The assistant, Troy, moves a signed photograph of his boss with Mark "Tubby" Taylor off a chair so that I can sit down.

"Mr Howard won't be a minute. Would you like a cup of tea?" Already, you can tell that this office is going to be like the pool-room in *The Castle*. Perhaps Howard, like several politicians I know with electorate offices that look like souvenir shops, isn't allowed to take this stuff home.

When Mr Howard appears, he looks exactly as he did when he was prime minister: neat and sprightly, with the distinct air of someone who has enjoyed an untroubled night's sleep. We step into a long room with a ridiculously nice view; this is clearly his private office, because the status of the people in the photographs tracks suddenly and exponentially upwards; the lobby might feature snaps of cricketers, but here in the inner sanctum it's strictly popes and queens and presidents.

What is immediately apparent about the former prime minister is that he is extraordinarily relaxed. There is little touchiness about him, and nothing at all by way of obvious pangs. Paul Keating, when asked after Rudd's election victory if he was happy to see the end of Howard, said: "Look how cautious people have got about, you know, this omnipresent government with its viciousness, you know? When it left it was like a ... I felt like ... you know sometimes you see people at factories, they've been in a plant that's got toxic stuff on them, they get hosed down later? I felt on Saturday night I'd been hosed down."

Defeat is still fresh for Howard, and yet it is difficult to envision him entertaining such hostility for his successor.

"Well, I lost the election, and I pretty quickly disengaged," he says, briskly. "The only interest I have in the party is wanting it to win."

I had last seen Howard in August 2008, at a Liberal Party dinner in western Sydney where hundreds of the faithful gathered among the usual clutter of display-framed Menzies handbills and Prime Minister's XI photographs (for the silent auction), to mourn the passing of their prime minister. Two of his backbench devotees, Pat Farmer and Louise Markus, were there to conduct the proceedings.

"I keep having to remind myself it's Mr Howard now," wailed Farmer, the Member for Macarthur, during his vote of thanks. "Not 'The Boss.' Not 'Prime Minister.' But you know what? No matter what happens, you'll always be the Prime Minister in my eyes."

Unable to bear the Member for Macarthur's raw grief, I glanced surreptitiously through the showbag that I'd found on my chair. It contained a tea-towel, a John Howard DVD, two energy-saver light bulbs, three Ferrero Rocher chocolates, a mini-bottle of Bundaberg rum and a copy of *Gourmet Traveller*'s January 2006 issue – a strikingly inappropriate collection of trinkets to commemorate the departure from public life of a man like John Howard.

In his influential 1973 essay "A Leader and a Philosophy," David Kemp (at that stage of his career, a very future Coalition minister) mounted a provocative argument about leadership.

"The first and most important relationship is between leader and followers, not between leader and the public," he wrote. Kemp was writing in January 1973, a month after Gough Whitlam bulldozed his way through the shambolic ranks of Billy McMahon's Liberal government in the "It's Time" election. The article – which paved the way for the ascent of Kemp's mentor, Malcolm Fraser, to the leadership – argued that too much had been made, in the past, of image and fuzzy notions of electoral appeal in the business of selecting Liberal leaders.

"Seeing leadership in terms of 'image' misses its most important ingredient," Kemp wrote. "The leader's first task is – as the very word implies

– to *lead* the party he leads. The ultimate support of a leader's authority is his role as expounder of a philosophy or ideology which commands common consent and adherence in the party."

In Kemp's model, the existence of a philosophy itself is the crucial thing, regardless of its detail or tint.

John Howard disagrees with Kemp, maintaining that the most important relationship is between a leader and voters, rather than the leader and his or her political tribe. Howard's own relationship with the electorate over eleven and a half years in government was a very precious thing to him. Like any intimate relationship, it took work. He liked to keep the lines of communication direct, favouring talkback radio above other media as a chance to commune directly with the beloved. This minimised any opportunity for Shakespearean confusion brought about by mischievous intermediaries.

It cost money, too, this relationship. Howard was forever splashing out on expensive trinkets to keep the month of the populace's infatuation ever May, to the serious frustration of his treasurer, Peter Costello.

He wasn't above serious policy U-turns, if he thought it would help. And even now, at the end of the affair, you can tell he thinks it's not really over. During the course of our conversation, Howard offers the following thought: "When you lose, the nature of things in politics is you think there has to be some immediate explanation as to why you lose an election. There wasn't an explanation for us because we were defeated at a time when the economy was running very strongly. When the incumbent prime minister was still personally quite popular."

"Still personally quite popular." In the mind of a true romantic, a love affair never really ends, does it? And even after losing government and being rolled out of his own seat, the former PM can't acknowledge that the magic is gone.

The *Sydney Morning Herald*'s political editor, Peter Hartcher, documents in his new book, *To The Bitter End*, the various approaches that were made to John Howard over the course of his final term suggesting that he should call it quits. The Liberal Party's pollster, Mark Textor – who had acted as a sort of matchmaker for Howard at the beginning of his affair with the Australian people – now tried tactfully to explain to Howard that it was coming to an end.

"But they like me," Hartcher reports Howard as insisting.

"Yes, but they want you to go," Textor would reply.

Easy for Howard to see his primary relationship as being with the voters, not his colleagues. But Howard is in fact a powerful example of David Kemp's point. Howard's period in the prime ministership encompasses a most fascinating episode in the history of leader–follower relations in the Liberal Party.

When the Coalition won power in 1996, thirty-six new Liberal, National Party and Country Liberal MPs won the privilege of heading to Canberra. Of that thirty-six, twenty-eight had won seats from the Labor Party. Rather surprised new MPs they were too, in some cases. Many of them had been preselected under the leadership of Alexander Downer, a difficult period during which dire predictions were made about the party remaining in Opposition for decades.

Having lost the unloseable election in 1993, the Liberal Party was not widely fancied to take government in 1996. So the Liberal preselection committees were hardly flooded with applications.

Warren Entsch, the former crocodile hunter, joined the Liberal Party on the same day he put his form in for preselection for the Queensland seat of Leichhardt. Sharman Stone, in order to run as a Liberal in the Victorian seat of Murray (held until 1996 by the Nationals), had to set up a Liberal Party branch just to nominate. Elizabeth Grace, a Queensland teacher and mother of adult children, was the only applicant for Liberal preselection in the seat of Lilley. She won the seat from Wayne Swan with a swing of 6.9 per cent. And Paul Marek, a coalminer who won the Queensland seat of Capricornia for the Liberals, could not be found for days after the election; he had gone back to the mines without even checking the result, assuming there was no way he would be elected. When located and informed that he had achieved a 6.9 per cent swing and was therefore the new Member for Capricornia, Marek was upset that his new job would involve a substantial pay cut.

Commonly, the "Class of 1996" featured small-business people with no background in politics who were angry with Paul Keating. It turned out that voters – on the whole – agreed. Warren Entsch won Leichhardt with a swing of 4.18 per cent. Other, even longer shots came romping home. In 1994, who would have dreamed that the western suburbs Sydney seat of Lindsay, Labor's by a margin of 10.22 per cent, would fall to the Liberal Party? But Jackie Kelly nabbed it with a swing of nearly 12 per cent, to her great amazement.

"I had a mobile phone and just waited for the phone to ring to find out what a federal member did," she later recalled.

This collection of new Coalition MPs was not a trivial addition to the parliamentary community in 1996: they made up nearly a quarter of sitting MPs. Paul A. Pickering's fascinating academic paper "The Class of 96: A Biographical Analysis of New Government Members of the Australian House of Representatives" describes the cultural and demographic change that these new MPs brought to their own party. Pickering compared the Class of 1996 to the similarly sized influx of Coalition MPs that flooded into Canberra after the rout of the Whitlam government in 1975.

The Class of 1975 had no women, and its inductees had come to conservative politics through predictable channels. "Of the 1975 cohort all but a handful were old boys of one of Australia's exclusive private schools including three graduates of Scotch College, two from Melbourne Grammar, two from Sydney Grammar and one each from Wesley, Xavier, Marcellin, Prince Alfred, Lindfield, Geelong Grammar, Canberra Grammar, Brisbane Grammar and Brighton Grammar," Pickering wrote. "Among the 'Class of '96,' by contrast, there is only one graduate of any of the above schools (Larry Anthony) and one or two others who attended a private school. For the most part they are graduates of run-of-the-mill State and Catholic Secondary Schools."

The 1996 inductees, twelve of whom were women, were much more likely to come from working-class backgrounds and from small business than their 1975 forebears. They were occupied with questions of bureaucracy and frustration for small business.

And overwhelmingly, they were motivated by family. While the topic of "the family" – as distinct from the inevitable and copious thanking of family members – was not mentioned once in the maiden speeches of the Class of 1975, it was mentioned 134 times in the maiden speeches of 1996, according to Pickering's analysis. Small business was mentioned 100 times.

The 1996 election, it is now clear, changed not only the fortunes of the Liberal Party, but also its face.

"There is no stereotypical Liberal," Jackie Kelly told the House of Representatives in her maiden speech. "The people here with me today are from all walks of life: housewives, social workers, businesswomen, people from the military, married, single, childless, people with eight kids, grown-up kids, grandkids and kids under five. Whatever the Bell curve in society is, it is reflected here in John Howard's government."

Howard himself says that the Class of '96 was notable for bringing a new strain to the Liberal Party. "I mean they had some association with the Liberal Party, but they were almost a breed apart," he says.

The new arrivals changed the culture of the party in a way which complemented Howard's own instincts and prejudices. The first budget's swingeing cuts to the university sector established a settled bitterness toward Howard there, and he reciprocated by promoting vocational education and encouraging youngsters to undertake apprenticeships. Over time, it became a popular mantra within the parliamentary party that university education was not all that it was cracked up to be.

"Minister Rates Trade As Valuable As Degree," read the headline on a Courier Mail news story on 25 November 2004. The article reported on some comments from the employment and training minister, the '96er Gary Hardgrave: "People with trade skills have all the power in the economy these days," he told the paper. "Unfortunately the psychology of the day is that if you haven't got a degree you must be a dud. But the shortages mean that a trade qualification is as good as a PhD and would probably earn you more."

George Brandis, an Oxford-educated barrister, rose in the party room not long after the article appeared and questioned Howard directly on it. He was all in support of trade qualifications, he said, but was it really now the government's position that a hairdressing certificate was as good as a PhD?

As he asked his question, Brandis was heckled by some of his colleagues, who jeered that people with degrees weren't as smart as they thought they were.

"He was howled down, of course. It was frightening," recalls one (university-educated) MP who was present. "They were a mob by that stage. You couldn't just get up and say things like that. It was like the French Revolution."

Howard himself, recalls another Liberal, made it clear where his sympathies lay. "He just gave out this big laugh, and said: 'Oh, George. At least you have more chance of making some money with a hairdressing certificate.'"

This scene came only months after the 2004 election campaign, during which Howard and his ministers had regularly criticised as "class warfare" the Labor Party's plans to strip government funding from Australia's most expensive private schools. That Howard could simultaneously denigrate university elites while defending high-school elites is a striking demonstration of his powers.

What caused this cultural shift within the Liberal Party? The eye goes where it is drawn: Howard brought the Class of '96 into parliament and they cleaved to him. It must be about Howard, you'd think. But many of the '96ers were preselected under Downer. If we return to the maiden speeches of those inductees, a common theme emerges: a shared motivation that drove this disparate band to down tools, pencils and in one case actual crocodiles to join the Liberal Party and seek political office.

Pickering takes up the story:

> When looking for common themes and motivations, any student of
> the thirty-six first speeches will be struck by the extent to which
> their authors appear to have been politicised by the experience of
> Labor in office. The list of Labor's crimes is long. For thirteen years
> Labor had: "failed the Australian people" (Kay Elson); restricted
> growth and "established bureaucratic barriers" (Mal Brough);
> "stopped listening to people" (Graeme McDougall); was "hide-
> bound, unresponsive, unsympathetic, unrepresentative and too
> busy playing political football to listen to the ordinary battler"
> (Jackie Kelly); had "forgotten about real people" (Gary Hardgrave);
> and, attacked "every revered institution in society – from the family
> through to the church and judiciary" (Tony Smith). And on it goes.
> "Our foreign debt skyrocketed and interest rates soared … the
> chasm between the haves and the have-nots … widened dramati-
> cally" (Ricky Johnston). Reflecting their origins perhaps, some even
> go as far as to lecture the Labor Party for having failed to uphold the
> traditional objectives of the Labour movement. For example, Bob
> Baldwin told the House that his late father "would surely turn in his
> grave at what Labor has done." A former union official, Paul Marek,
> declared that "control of unions must be given back to the rank and
> file … [They] are sick to death of the high fliers of the union move-
> ment trying to coerce branch members into embarking upon indus-
> trial campaigns of a political nature."

Is it possible that this marked cultural change within the Liberal Party
of Australia could be Paul Keating's doing?

Howard never missed an opportunity to trumpet the defection of blue-
collar Australia from Labor to the Coalition, and the classmates of '96
were an excellent illustration of his point. These MPs owed their political
careers to Howard, and they felt that their fortunes were inextricably
entwined with his. Many of them learned everything they knew about

politics from their leader. Perhaps it's helpful to think of them as political ducklings: hatching out into the world of politics, they bonded with the first parental figure they saw – John Howard.

As Howard prevailed again and again in political crisis after political crisis, their respect for him only grew, and few of them entertained any notion of another leader.

"They formed a poultice of support for John Howard, over a long period of time," says Nelson of his '96 classmates. "He had a special place in their world, and they had a special place in his."

The Class of 1996 proved to be political stayers of some tenacity. At the 1998 election, eleven of them fell, but three of those – Don Randall, Bob Baldwin and Russell Broadbent – clawed their way back in subsequent elections. By 2007, eleven years after their arrival in Canberra, a healthy twenty-three of the original thirty-six remained.

From New South Wales, there was Gary Nairn, Joanna Gash, Danna Vale, Jackie Kelly, Kerry Bartlett, Joe Hockey, Jim Lloyd, Brendan Nelson and the National Party's Ian Causley. From Queensland: Peter Lindsay, Warren Entsch, Teresa Gambaro, Mal Brough, Kay Elson and De-Anne Kelly (also from the Nationals). There was Phil Barresi, Russell Broadbent and Sharman Stone from Victoria, South Australians Andrew Southcott and Trish Draper, and the West Australian Don Randall.

Of these MPs (discounting, of course, the Nationals), only a handful would have voted for Peter Costello in a party-room spill: Joe Hockey, Phil Barresi, Andrew Southcott and possibly Sharman Stone. In political terms, the Class of 1996 functioned as an effective Praetorian guard for John Howard for more than eleven years – quite a marvel. While they did not account for more than 50 per cent of the Coalition party room, they were numerous enough to offer substantial resistance to Peter Costello, or anyone else with pretensions to the throne.

Nor did Costello try especially hard to woo them. He thought many of the '96ers were fools – an opinion of which they were sharply aware. Whereas Howard duchessed these MPs, made regular and tender solicitations of their opinions and staged an annual dinner in their honour, Costello avoided them.

Jackie Kelly sought revenge in 2006, in an interview with Maxine McKew, just before McKew stopped being a journalist and started being the challenger for John Howard's seat.

"The Labor Party for decades before I came on the scene would say, 'No, you don't want to be a Liberal because they are this twin-set and pearls lot off the North Shore and they are nasty, terribly unfeeling, uncharitable, toffee-nosed rich people," Kelly told the ABC. "I broke the mould – John Howard as well. Whereas I think Peter still suffers from that; they can just pigeonhole him and say, 'Yeah, those nasty Liberals you don't want to be a part of.'"

Costello, as you might imagine, did not appreciate being told indirectly that he was a "toffee-nosed rich person." Particularly not by Jackie Kelly, who by then owned seven homes with her orthodontist husband and was building an eighth. His impatience with Kelly is apparent in his memoir, when he describes the episode that marked her swan-song in Lindsay: with days to go before the 2007 election, Kelly's husband and some other men were caught handing out racist pamphlets jigged up to look like ALP campaign literature. Kelly stumbled her way through an excruciating live interrogation about the incident, broadcast by the ABC the next morning, the "call interruption" beeps audible on the phone line deeply suggestive of a desperate adviser trying to get through and tell her to shut up. In his memoir, Costello records himself as shouting at his car radio: "Why do these people give interviews?"

Just as it became the vogue within the Liberal Party to decry university education, it became an orthodoxy that political professionals – people who had worked as staff members or officials within the party – made for less desirable MPs than "ordinary people" who had knocked around a bit.

"It was a land where the non-politician was king," recalls one MP. "Where the Bob Baldwins and the Jackie Kellys were regarded as the smart people, because they could win seats. And the political hacks were the idiots, because they didn't understand how ordinary people thought."

Howard's version of events is necessarily more moderate. "I would never have denigrated the role of political professionals," he says. "But I did not want parliament to be full of people whose previous experience had been as political staffers. I had a very strong concern that we would end up with politics on both sides being dominated by people whose whole careers had been in politics. Political astuteness is not measured by the length of time you've worked in politics. I think the best combination for the Liberal Party – and that was why I wanted to see Turnbull come in – I wanted to see people whose life experiences had been a mix of politics from an early age but who had spent a dozen or so years doing something else." The optimum experience he describes here, consciously or unconsciously, is very precisely his own: Howard was involved in the Liberal Party from an early age, then practised as a solicitor for twelve years before entering parliament.

By and large, Howard got his wish: a party room richly supplied with real people, who had a pleasing additional tendency to agree with everything he said. Of course, no such stability would have been possible without Howard's own deep policy convictions, which became the policy convictions of the government. After all, as the Bible reminds readers in Corinthians: "For if the trumpet give an uncertain sound, who shall prepare himself to the battle?"

The downsides to unhesitating adulation are never immediately apparent to its recipient. That's the difficulty with sycophants – they're handy, and the chances are that at some point in the cycle they were even right about your genius. But you can't just go on believing them forever, and for John Howard, you could fairly say that the Class of 1996 was incredibly helpful right up to the point at which it became incredibly unhelpful. This tipping point came at about the time when it would have been sensible for John Howard and the Liberal Party to effect a leadership transition.

For many years, John Howard's leadership formula was hard-wired to an institutional truism: "I will stay for as long as my party wants me to stay." Even now he invokes it, in discussing Peter Costello: "As far as he and I were concerned, the reality was that the party never wanted to change to him. They were never within a bull's roar of wanting to do that."

Brendan Nelson agrees: "You've also got to remember that as far as John staying, he continued to be there because the party room believed on balance that John was preferable to Peter. The majority view in 2006, when it came to a head with the McLachlan note, was 'Yes, we know that John's been there for a long time, yes we know that it's probably time for change, but we respect the job that John Howard is doing and we respect his right to keep doing it if he wants to keep doing it.'"

The party room, in other words, politely ceded its authority right back to Howard, who decided to stay on.

A very similar thing happened to the cabinet in September 2007, when the world's leaders gathered in Sydney for the APEC conference and the Australian government put on an unscheduled but spectacular show of self-destruction. As has been widely reported, Howard developed a wobble at this time about his ability to hold government or even his seat at the fast-approaching federal election. So he sent Alexander Downer out to canvass the views of the cabinet. Downer convened a late-night meeting in his hotel room, the cloak-and-dagger nature of which, one imagines, cannot but have appealed to some of them, particularly the Member for Wentworth. The majority of cabinet attendees voiced the opinion that it would be better for Howard to go – especially if he himself was having doubts about his viability.

When Downer relayed the message to Howard, the prime minister sent a message back: he would go, but only if the cabinet itself, by means of its individual ministers, directly asked him to resign. Howard told Peter Hartcher that in his view the ministers had to "accept the responsibility for these sorts of things. I mean, I think some of them wanted a situation where I would just disappear. They would not in any way be held responsible for it, and then, if it all blew up, well, then, 'We didn't ask John to go.' I mean, I don't know, but you can't operate that way."

One is vaguely reminded of the exchange between Malcolm Turnbull and Conrad Black, all those years ago.

Turnbull: If you want to be an assassin, you have got to get blood on your hands.

Black: You don't just want me to have blood on my hands, you want my bloody fingerprints on the dagger.

Very well, then – Howard wanted his cabinet's bloody fingerprints on the dagger, and in the end they were too squeamish, so let it rest. The ministers, too, ceded their authority back to Howard, who chose to stay on.

John Howard had, by then, been a Liberal MP for three decades, and for much of that time – a long stint during the 1980s and 1990s – he had excelled in leadership manoeuvring. In 2007's half-baked coup, it quickly became clear that there was only one Liberal MP who was any good at leadership contests, and he was already the leader.

The cabinet members, challenged by Howard to put up or shut up, shut up. Only two of them – Mal Brough and Joe Hockey – took up Howard's invitation and asked him directly to stand down. Andrew Robb, though not in the cabinet, approached Howard separately at about this time and told him point-blank that he should go. Nick Minchin says that he conveyed a message to Howard to the same effect, though Howard denies receiving it. And Malcolm Turnbull, it should be acknowledged, had already told Howard mid-year that Howard was "in danger of becoming the problem" for the government.

It is telling that the "political professionals" in the Howard ministry – former federal director Robb, former staffer and factional boss Hockey, and long-term party officebearer Nick Minchin – were so strongly represented in the scanty ranks of those who sought Howard's departure. Of the ranks of the "real people," only two – Mal Brough and Malcolm Turnbull – took that step.

The APEC episode is a particularly earthy reminder of the nature of politics: a chancy business full of loose ends and missed calls. For all the appearance of fierce organisation, and for all that its stalkings and garrottings bear the superficial hallmarks of intelligent design, politics is a game played by humans, with all the mess that entails. If the cabinet had pushed a bit harder, if Howard had been a bit clearer, things could have unfolded differently. But they didn't.

"The first and most important relationship is between leader and followers, not between leader and the public," insisted David Kemp. John Howard might not agree with Kemp, but it's plain that Howard's relationship with his own followers within the parliamentary Liberal Party constituted both his greatest strength in the business of maintaining power, and his greatest weakness in the business of its graceful relinquishment.

The voters having done the job instead, where does this leave Malcolm Turnbull? With an internal image problem. The model of the effective Liberal politician that evolved over the Howard years – not too flashy, not too university-educated, not too rich – doesn't leave much room for Turnbull, with his exuberant millions and his Oxonian refinements. Having spent more than a decade getting comfortable in the raiment of the Howard battlers, can you blame what's left of Howard's party for its wariness of someone who so demonstrably is not a battler?

The Liberal Party of today wears Malcolm Turnbull like a borrowed suit. The suit looks fine – it's a lovely suit, it's not that. But the wearer is forever tugging and fretting, and worrying that it's overdressed. And wondering what people will think, and thinking very frequently of its old suit – the one that was thrown out – and its second-best suit, which went to the dry-cleaner's some time ago and hasn't yet come back. The suit, in the manner of suits, does its best to give where it can, but there's a limit to how much it can change, and anyway it doesn't really see the problem. It's a suit, and it is what it is. The question is this: after fifteen years in Roger David, can the Liberal Party ever get comfortable in borrowed Brioni?

Turnbull's talk of childhood hardship and growing up in a flat doesn't help much, either. It might be true, but it doesn't sit very believably on Turnbull, whose moneyed glow at fifty-five is absolutely unmistakeable, no matter how many Vegemite-sandwich dinners he ate when he was thirteen. "Kevin Rudd is just as wealthy as I am," Turnbull regularly complains to colleagues, and confronted with the brute digits most Australians would probably concur, given that after the first $50 million most of us stop bothering with matters of degree. But Rudd doesn't ooze it in the way that Turnbull does; another of life's little injustices.

There is, of course, a powerful modern vogue for log-cabin stories in public life. Kevin Rudd, as anyone who follows politics would by now exhaustedly concede, lost his father at eleven and recalls sleeping in a car with his family afterwards, as the widowed Mrs Rudd battled to find a new home for her brood. Brendan Nelson recalls accompanying his father as a child on walks through wealthy neighbourhoods in Tasmania, on which excursion certain pithy paternal observations were delivered about what it meant to have money, and why the Nelsons didn't have any. Is it any wonder that poor Kim Beazley, who was burdened with two loving parents and a sturdy roof over his head, never seemed to get anywhere?

The easiest way of putting all this is that the times do not suit Malcolm Turnbull. Not in the Liberal Party, which has adopted the shape of John Howard and will take some time to relax into a new one. And not in the broader community, where opinion polls increasingly indicate that Turnbull is either ignored or dismissed.

Anyone with a little knowledge of political cycles could have foreseen that leadership at this early stage of Opposition, against a strongly performing government, was going to be extraordinarily difficult. Were Turnbull less impetuous, he might have waited a term or two; sustained observation of Peter Costello tends to lend weight to the suspicion that that is what he is doing. If Turnbull finds that the times do not suit him, he has no-one to blame but himself. But Turnbull has never baulked at any hurdle, real or imagined. Stop at nothing. The idea that he might delay his ambitions to accommodate something as insignificant as a political cycle is simply unrealistic.

His comparative public unpopularity presents a considerable difficulty inside the party for Turnbull, whose criticism of Brendan Nelson as leader was so strongly based on Nelson's poor popularity ratings that he cannot possibly avoid having the argument turned neatly back on him now by his colleagues. Turnbull expected to be doing much better than he is; so did many of his colleagues when they elected him leader, and the fact that he isn't is a big problem.

Why is Turnbull not doing better? It's not that he makes blunders; he doesn't, as a rule. And his concerns about the Rudd government's dash into debt are hardly a boutique criticism. Plenty of people worry about the mountain of debt presently being assembled for their children, and Turnbull's should by rights be a compelling voice of opposition. There are a couple of reasons for the failure; depressingly for Turnbull, there's not much he can do about any of them.

First, Rudd's electoral supremacy seems particularly bulletproof at present. At a time of crisis, the image of a hyperactive prime minister shovelling everything he can at the advancing financial crisis seems to have wide appeal. Rudd's robotic gift for jargon has a unique capacity to annoy. But there is no doubt that he is a master of political messaging, due to his discipline and preparedness to repeat stock phrases again and again in what is sometimes called the "vomit" principle; as in, keep saying it until you want to vomit and you are pretty sure everyone else wants to, too. "Decisive action," "ahead of the eight-ball" and "cushioning the blow" are some of Rudd's greatest hits from the Global Financial Crisis vomitorium.

Note, too, that Rudd's superior messaging service is already churning out some very targeted material on Turnbull. Negative, negative, negative, the message goes. Turnbull's always carping. Isn't interested in saving Australia from financial meltdown. Can't stand to agree with someone else's ideas.

The way ahead is not without hope for Turnbull. Things can change quickly in politics, especially in a period of swift global change. As Rudd and his colleagues proceed further and further down the path of public debt, an ideological divide opens wider and wider between the two parties, and Turnbull's small-government mantra is necessarily afforded more room to be heard. Turnbull has laid strong groundwork for this possibility by opposing the government's $43 billion stimulus expenditure early this year.

Secondly, Turnbull suffers – as so many Opposition leaders have before him, especially his immediate predecessor – from insurrection in his own ranks. Such insurrection drains a leader of strength, and thrives most strongly when there is a figure around which it can coalesce. That figure, at present, is Peter Costello, who never did depart for that career in the corporate world and whose ongoing presence alone is sufficient to keep certain Liberal hearts aflutter with hope that he might soon be prepared to lead. This is an odd sort of threat to Turnbull, and not at all the kind of fight with which he is most at home. Costello is a passive aggressor; his career has been spent waiting until conditions are right. The threat he presents now is entirely nebulous – a question mark, a possibility only. For Turnbull, whose three standard responses to threat (attack it head-on, sue it or throw money at it) are useless in this situation, there is very little he can do. Turnbull is an impatient person, and despises what he sees as Costello's cowardice. But such is Turnbull's stubbornness that one suspects he would use his last breath to thwart Costello.

"Malcolm's an optimist," is how George Brandis puts it, and it is a perceptive observation. But optimism seems a quaint indulgence at the moment, doesn't it? Like Turnbull himself, optimism doesn't seem to fit the epoch. In so many ways, Turnbull is a politician constructed for prosperity; for the golden years. For building libraries and studying the twelve great cultures and being funny and interesting and knowing who Pliny was. It's hard to doubt his enthusiasm for Australia, or his love for it. There are many things that are endearing about Malcolm Turnbull, not least his persistent and misguided belief that politics is a meritocracy.

But this is a time of recession. *Laissez-faire* is an attractive approach for the times when you are reasonably certain that the *faire* bit will involve more ups than downs, on balance. Turnbull's guiding political and philosophical ethos, which is one of non-intervention, is perfect for fair weather, but tends to get lost in foul, which is one of the reasons for his difficulty in making himself heard. Politics is about timing, most of the old hands will tell you, and they are not wrong.

SOURCES

6   "Initiated by Turnbull!": Graham Richardson, "The Man Who Would Be King," *The Bulletin*, 28 October 2003, p. 30.

8   "Paul Keating, that savage verbal caricaturist, said": Eleanor Hall, interview with Paul Keating, *The World Today*, 26 November 2007.

10   "Turnbull wrote grandly in 1999, on the origins of his republican odyssey": Malcolm Turnbull, *Fighting For The Republic*, Hardie Grant: Melbourne, 1999, p. 2.

12   "Charles Moore, editor of *The Spectator* from 1984 to 1990, wrote in 2003": "I Don't Want Your Cash, Mr Murdoch," *The Independent*, 23 September 2003.

19   "Malcolm Turnbull (at nineteen) wrote in his student newspaper": Malcolm Turnbull, "Gough Whitlam," *Honi Soit* 26, 1974, p. 5.

24   "John Howard, for instance, speaking about his university years": Patrick O'Brien, *The Liberals: Factions, Feuds and Fancies*, Viking: Melbourne, 1985, p. 84.

24   "as he put it, 'a leftish weekly called *Nation Review*'": Malcolm Turnbull, *The Spycatcher Trial*, Heinemann Australia: Melbourne, 1988, p. 2.

24   "As he put it: 'I was serving, simultaneously, Marx, God and Mammon'": ibid.

25   "Tony Abbott … promptly organised a pro-Kerr rally": Michael Duffy, *Latham and Abbott*, Random House: Sydney, 2004, p. 34.

28   "wrote Ellis of Turnbull and Keating's shared fascination": Bob Ellis, "An Honourable, Fidgetty, Humanist Liberalism," ABC *Unleashed*, <www.abc.net.au/unleashed/stories/s2107621.htm>, 3 December 2007.

29   "published an article on [Lang] in 1992": Mark Latham, "The Forgotten Land," *The Hummer*, publication of the Sydney Branch, Australian Society for the Study of Labour History, April–August, 1992, p. 121.

29   "wrote an obituary of Lang in 1975": Malcolm Turnbull, "Lang: A Man Who Knew How To Hate," *Nation Review*, 3–9 October 1975, p. 1299.

32   "the unbowdlerised account": Conrad Black, *A Life In Progress*, Key Porter Books: Toronto, 1993, p. 436.

32   "cited his artist colleague Ward O'Neill's drawing of Turnbull": Alan Ramsey, "Malcolm, The Mogul and Moggy Myths," *Sydney Morning Herald*, 20 September 2008.

33   "'Malcolm is really a pussycat,' mused the broadcaster Phillip Adams": John Lyons, "Raging Turnbull," *Good Weekend*, 13 April 1991, p. 21.

34   "Jim McClelland, who in 1991 had this to say of Turnbull": ibid.

34   "nothing better than gutter abuse": ibid.

38   "'violent public attack on Costigan,' is how Turnbull described his tactics": Malcolm Turnbull, *The Spycatcher Trial*, op. cit., p. 7.

43   "'lack of respect for our opponents,' Turnbull later admitted": ibid., p. 15.

43   "How do we get onto [the British Labour leader, Neil] Kinnock?": ibid., p. 27–28.

44   "Turnbull's own account of the conversation illustrates": ibid., p. 117.

46   "told *The Sydney Morning Herald* in 1990": Interview with Marian Wilkinson and Paul Syvret, *Sydney Morning Herald*, 22 September 1990.

46   "To *The Age* he explained": John Sampson, "Media Casualty," *The Age*, 23 September 1990.

46   "his legal column for *The Bulletin*": Malcolm Turnbull, "The Law," *The Bulletin*, 14 July 1981.

46   "Mum's next book": Coral Lansbury, *The Old Brown Dog: Women, Workers and Vivisection in Edwardian England*, University of Wisconsin Press, 1985.

49   "account of the Fairfax affair": Colleen Ryan and Glenn Burge, *Corporate Cannibals: The Taking Of Fairfax*, Mandarin Australia: Melbourne, 1993, p. 74.

50   "*Chutzpah* is a wonderful Yiddish word": Malcolm Turnbull, "PM's Cheap Money Shot," *The Weekend Australian*, 7–8 March 2009.

51   "he told *Good Weekend* equably in 1988, aged 33": Suellen O'Grady, "What Malcolm Wants, Malcolm Gets," *Good Weekend*, 3 September 1988, p. 60.

54   "Conrad Black … later wrote of Turnbull": Conrad Black, op. cit., p. 436.

55   "he told *Good Weekend* in 1988": Suellen O'Grady, op. cit., p. 60.

66   "he told Fran Kelly late last year": Interview with Fran Kelly, *Radio National Breakfast*, 28 November 2007.

74   "Turnbull gave an interview to Fran Kelly": ibid.

77   "an interview with the *Courier Mail*": Clinton Porteous, "Malcolm Turnbull says Kevin Rudd is odd, very undiplomatic and chilly," *The Courier Mail*, 8 November 2008.

80   "Paul Keating, when asked after Rudd's election victory": Interview with Eleanor Hall, *The World Today*, op. cit.

81   "In his influential 1973 essay": David Kemp, "A Leader And A Philosophy," *Checkpoint*, Vol. 13, 1973, pp. 3–13.

82   "documents in his new book": Peter Hartcher, *To the Bitter End: The Dramatic Story Behind the Fall of John Howard and the Rise of Kevin Rudd*, Allen & Unwin: Crow's Nest, NSW, 2009, p. 218.

84   "'what a federal member did,' she later recalled": Interview with Jackie Kelly by Maxine McKew, *Sunday Profile*, ABC Local Radio, 6 August 2006.

84   "Paul A. Pickering's fascinating academic paper": Paul A. Pickering, "The

Class of '96: A Biographical Analysis of New Government Members of the Australian House of Representatives," *Australian Journal of Politics and History*, Vol. 44, No. 1, March 1998, pp. 95–112.

84   "Of the 1975 cohort all but a handful were old boys": ibid., p. 100.

87   "When looking for common themes and motivations": ibid., p. 103.

89   "Jackie Kelly sought revenge in 2006, in an interview": Interview with Maxine McKew, op. cit.

89   "Costello records himself as shouting at his car radio": Peter Costello and Peter Coleman, *The Costello Memoirs*, Melbourne University Press, 2008, p. 2.

Patrice Newell

Guy Pearse's *Quarterly Essay* builds on his massive and important *High and Dry* (Penguin, 2007). Given his erstwhile status as a Liberal insider – working in the belly of the beast – he can reveal the depth of Howard's climate-change denialism and give the names, ranks and serial numbers of the greenhouse mafia that successfully derailed the ideal of sustainable progress. Now we see how powerful that lobby remains in the era of Rudd and Wong.

Pearse is a first-class researcher, dogged and courageous. He unearths facts like a miner following a seam. In the case of *Quarry Vision* he quarries a vast number of cited sources. And the revelations pile up, identifying the miscreants. (We learn that X and Y and Z left the ministry to get jobs in the mining industry, with Z scoring a well-paid directorship of mining company A.)

Recently Rudd's new parliamentary secretary for climate change, Greg Combet (member for Charlton), spoke at a local meeting in northern New South Wales. Environmental chat rooms ran hot with the revelation that Combet was unfamiliar with James Hansen. The Australian prime minister's new adviser hadn't heard of NASA's leading climate scientist?

We now know where Combet's ignorance begins. But where does it end? Thankfully Combet has political skills – we saw them during the waterfront dispute. It's imperative and urgent that he gets up to speed on this issue and fights. He could learn from Graham Richardson. Richo, the classic "fixer," was a potent environment minister.

The central problem for the best-intentioned politicians is posed by the central question, "How do we get there from here?" While Rudd may well dream of getting to 100 per cent renewable energy in 2020 or fantasise about being a world leader on climate change, he doesn't seem to have any idea *how* to get there. He seems bogged in caution – overwhelmed by the limitations of power in an arena of big money, big government revenues and a convergence of trade-union and corporate resistance.

This cautious approach to climate-change reform is in fact the riskiest. The failing big three car makers offer a convincing lesson. Propping up last century's energy system prohibits new innovations from gaining momentum.

The Australian Industry Group calculates that a $20 per tonne carbon price would increase the cost of goods and services by 0.9 per cent and yet businesses are screaming for government aid, claiming they will be uncompetitive internationally. But the Australian dollar fell by 35 per cent in three months last year and two years before that rose by 35 per cent. Entire industries can grow or be wiped out with such volatility. Whinging about a possible 0.9 per cent overall cost increase is unconvincing.

Politicians habitually associate with companies that generate cash flow. As well as filling their shareholders' coffers and government kitties, they are often the source of election donations. You see the dynamic most clearly in New South Wales, where the state government is addicted to coal. My research shows that no application to open or extend a coal mine in New South Wales has ever been denied – and there are more than seventeen currently queuing for approval as the miners march across the state, munching prime farmland and devouring river systems.

To paraphrase an old TV ad for oil, coal ain't just coal. It's used for two distinct purposes: making electricity and making steel. We know clean electricity alternatives abound: solar-photovoltaic and thermal, wind, hydro, geothermal and bio-mass are all poised to contribute. But steel production? That's another matter. The blast furnaces making steel use almost three times more coal than iron ore in the process, and the alternatives are harder to provide. So when anti-coal advocates crusade against coal, they must differentiate. The first target has to be thermal coal rather than metallurgical. We still need steel, if only to build giant windmills, solar installations and other components in the renewable-energy infrastructure.

It's coal mining for electricity that must be phased out.

To get there (to a non-carbon-polluting economy, i.e. a sustainable future) from here (Australia is the biggest per capita CO_2 polluter in the world) requires governments and political parties to free themselves from the gravitational pull of coal's easy money. If only governments didn't have to waste so much money on education, health care and public transport.

And where coal fills government coffers as it fills the coal trains heading to Newcastle and Gladstone, those pesky renewable-energy industries keep clamouring for funds. It seems private-sector investment must be seduced by tax incentives and matched by the public sector.

How do we get there from here?

After establishing a proper target to reduce emissions, that is, 25–40 per cent by 2020, let's start by reducing government expenditure on infrastructure for existing polluting industries.

April 2009 will be remembered for the contribution to the debate of the little-known Professor Peter Newman, from Infrastructure Australia, who urged Rudd to scrap the expansion of the coal-export capacity at Newcastle and deplored government spending on "clean" coal. Here was one of the PM's team saying what Al Gore, James Hansen and every climate-change crusader had been saying for years. Stop spending government money on both extending and underwriting the coal industry.

To get there from here, let's see Rudd, Wong and Combet table a plan for the total phasing out of Australia's coal-generated electricity. It may take decades but let's start.

Clean coal? If and when that turns from spin to science and coal-fired power stations can capture and store their pollution, we can renegotiate. But now, with the desperate need to reduce the amount of CO2 being pumped into the atmosphere, it is both reckless and immoral to keep bank-rolling thermal coal.

Let's see a national campaign educating us, the voters, on the true costs of climate change – not just a one-off event like the welcomed *Hidden Costs of Electricity* report recently launched by the minister for finance, Lindsay Tanner. I want to see a national TV campaign like the one we all endured when Howard was hard-selling the GST.

Let's cap and reduce our thermal-coal exports (for electricity generation overseas).

And let's not fall for the plan to offset Australia's pollution by reducing deforestation in Asia. It's an admirable idea – to reduce the burning of jungles and habitats. But in terms of energy policy this is fobbing off, not reform, and will only delay the restructure we need at home.

How to get there from here? It's not something Rudd can do on his own. Not while our constitution has the states responsible for land, water and energy. It's state governments that pretend to assess every exploration licence, mine plan, breach of condition and environmental complaint. For instance, in September 2008, in New South Wales, Invincible Colliery (Coalpac Pty Ltd) near Lithgow was found guilty of extracting 80 per cent more coal in a year than it was approved to do. Coalpac was fined $200,000. Imagine building your house 80 per cent bigger than your approved plan.

The list of coal mines breaching approval conditions is long and includes such complaints as over-extraction, dumping saline water into rivers, blasting when windy, noise pollution, cracking river beds, polluting streams and subsidence.

With the Rudd government endorsing the expansion of Gladstone and Newcastle ports and co-funding almost half of a $1.2 billion project to expand new rail lines for the Hunter Valley – solely for the purpose of transporting coal – why would a state government bother even thinking about reform?

Until change happens within a state's department of planning, quarry vision will continue to defeat the visionary. And negative climate change wins.

Patrice Newell

Bernard Keane

One of the more disconcerting aspects of Guy Pearse's *Quarry Vision* is the frighteningly *organic* way in which carbon dependence has been built into the Australian polity, as if its roots were every bit as deep as the coal we have so much invested in digging up. While much of the essay focuses on the success of climate sceptics and the carbon lobby under the Howard government, Pearse also stresses the success of the resources sector in influencing policy under both the Hawke-Keating government and, now, the Rudd government.

The failure of successive governments to understand the need for action to slow the growth of, and then reduce, carbon emissions has been a failure of Australia's entire governing class: its MPs, its public servants, its media of influence, its union and business leaders.

Such an observation is not intended to damn all members of that class, but to suggest that there has been a systemic failure as much as a moral and intellectual failure by particular individuals.

On balance, this failure is unusual in Australia in recent decades. Australia has been served by its governing class reasonably well since the early 1980s. Both the Hawke-Keating and Howard governments had their policy failures, and both, especially the latter, drifted to their deaths having lost all fiscal discipline. But the long period of economic growth recently concluded by the financial crisis — including an extended period of above-average productivity growth in the 1990s — was a direct consequence of a commitment to economic reform by Australia's most senior politicians, public servants, business and union leaders. In particular, the Hawke government's decisive abandonment of manufacturing protectionism, the Keating government's embrace of decentralised wage-fixing and competition policy, and the Howard government's reform of the taxation system were, probably in descending order, important elements in creating and sustaining the long economic boom Australia enjoyed after the recession of the early 1990s.

The abandonment of carbon protectionism, however, looks to be a reform too far for both sides of politics. The necessary but not sufficient characteristic of any major economic reform is genuine will on the part of governing officials to pursue it, based on an understanding of its long-term benefits. This leads to a willingness to accept the risk of short-term political damage in undertaking the reform, on the basis either that such long-term benefits will provide a political pay-off, or, as with Paul Keating or John Howard, that "good policy can be good politics." With Keating's once-in-a-generation political skills, economic reform was not merely less damaging politically, it actually became glamorous. And John Howard, despite the narrowness of his victory in 1998, was able to craft a GST reform agenda based on the perceived need for Australia to take its taxation medicine.

With a few exceptions, however, none of Australia's governing class genuinely accepts both the need for, and opportunities implicit in, the transition to a low-carbon economy.

Worse, the environment for serious policy debate in Australia has dramatically worsened in the last twenty years. Two factors have contributed significantly to this deterioration: the proliferation of "alternative" sources of policy advice, and the development of a permanent cadre of politically connected players.

The proliferation of sources of advice and opinion in any polity would, normally, be a welcome development. Until the 1980s, policy advice to governments was the preserve – indeed, the monopoly – of the Australian public service, especially given the lack of ministerial staff. Staffers began proliferating in the early 1980s. Think-tanks – usually but not invariably conservative – began emerging, with an explicit goal of influencing the political agenda. More importantly, the private sector entered the realm of policy research and development, and consultancies – large and small – working in public-sector fields of expertise began sprouting in Canberra, usually staffed by former public servants and ministerial advisers.

Consultants will always have an automatic advantage over public servants: they will provide whatever advice was asked for. Public servants had – and still have – an unfortunate tendency to call bad policy bad policy. Consultants aren't burdened by such recalcitrance. Again, this is not to condemn an entire profession. The majority of consultants are professional and intellectually rigorous. But they are also adept at sensing what is required by those who pay them, and what will generate repeat business. Ironically, they also come with the cache of being "independent," when of course they are anything but. Such "independence" proved enormously attractive to the Howard government. Senior bureaucrats and ministers quickly realised that the Howard Cabinet would be much more accepting of a proposal if it came backed by a report from an "independent consultant" rather than public servants.

The private sector quickly caught on to this trick, and these days it is a rare policy pitch from lobbyists that is not backed up by a glossy report from a prominent consultant. As a perfect case in point, the biggest beneficiaries of the emissions-trading debate in the last twelve months have been Canberra consultants – some of whom Pearse singles out – paid by polluting industries to offer analyses that suit the agenda of the polluters. Consider the career trajectory of Brian Fisher, the former head of the Australian Bureau of Agricultural and Resource Economics (ABARE). Fisher, latterly having joined right-wing economist and Liberal adviser Henry Ergas and former Howard staff at Concept Economics, was hired by the Minerals Council to prepare an independent analysis of Treasury's modelling of the impact of emissions trading. Fisher was then, remarkably, hired without any selection process by a Coalition-controlled Senate committee to continue his attack on Treasury's modelling at taxpayers' expense.

The proliferation of such "expert" opinions available for hire has dramatically lowered the quality of economic debate in Australia. The media remains oblivious – perhaps wilfully oblivious – to this. The claims of "independent" consultants and the outcomes of their modelling are reported without question. Most journalists, including those in the press gallery, lack an economics background and thus the capacity to question the material pumped out by industry, and lack sufficient understanding of the policy process to contextualise what they are being fed. Laziness or outright bias is another factor. In one case, the Minerals Council's claim, via Nationals senator Barnaby Joyce, that the government's emissions trading scheme would cost 50,000 mining jobs in Queensland was reported without demur in the house organ of climate scepticism, the *Australian*, when a quick check of ABS statistics would have shown there were actually fewer than 50,000 people in the entire Queensland mining sector.

Also slow to cotton on has been the environmental movement, which traditionally has been weak on both economics and an understanding of the policy process. The self-interested claims of industry have only rarely been contested, and more usually left on the public record as something approaching Holy Writ. In the circumstance where politicians may have been genuinely open-minded about the impact of climate change and the need for urgent action, there has been little balance to the spin and outright lies coming from industry and their modellers-for-hire.

Pearse also perceptively notes how many lobbyists for big polluters are former advisers to politicians, or politicians themselves. The development of consultancies, lobbying firms (including the new American-inspired trend of lobbying activities provided by legal and accounting firms) and the PR and government-relations arms of major companies and industry groups has established career paths for the politically connected that simply did not exist two decades ago.

It is now a well-worn career path for men and women to move from the youth wings of their respective parties or, in the case of ALP members, the trade-union movement, into ministerial offices as advisers, into parliament once preselection is secured, or into lobbying or government relations, with occasional detours into journalism, PR or a senior public-service position. This means Australia's political class grows ever more incestuous and uniform in its views, even if those aligned with parties currently in opposition have limited access to power (the reason why the most successful lobbying firms have representatives from both sides of politics in their senior ranks). Those with the best connections expect, and obtain, access at the most senior level. Political donations smooth the way. The Australian Petroleum Production & Exploration Association (APPEA), headed by former senior Commonwealth public servant Belinda Robinson and represented in Canberra by high-profile lobbyists Parker and Partners, paid the Labor Business Forum $15,000 for a table at a fundraiser on the anniversary of Labor's election victory last November – while Cabinet was determining the details of industry-compensation arrangements in the emissions trading scheme White Paper. The White Paper extended compensation to a number of APPEA members.

These structural features of Australia's governing class mean that a genuine debate on the need to address climate change is currently impossible. Future generations have no lobbyists; the environment hires no consulting firms; while polluters bring the heaviest policy artillery to bear.

Yet this is slowly changing. The Climate Institute – the target of criticism from much of the environmental movement – is devoting significant resources to economic research on the emissions trading scheme and climate-change issues. The Australian Conservation Foundation has done excellent work revealing the extraordinary generosity to big polluters of the government's proposed ETS. Industries that stand to lose – or are already losing – jobs as a consequence of climate change are speaking up about the real job losses consequent to a business-as-usual approach. But far more needs to be done to make the policy debate a genuine and informed contest rather than one heavily biased in favour of those with the deepest pockets.

One of the most significant changes in the debate has been the Garnaut Review. While Pearse, and others, criticise Garnaut's conclusions and targets, they overlook the fact that Garnaut's work established an economically credible case for action on climate change. After Garnaut, there is nowhere for anyone with economic credibility to hide on climate change. Instead, sceptics and rent-seekers had to switch their argument to one of timing, urging delay until the rest of the world – and in particular India and China – agreed to take action.

The reaction from advocates of climate-change action has been to argue that Australia must take action both on moral and diplomatic grounds: that as the beneficiary of 200 years of carbon-based industrialisation, we cannot fairly demand that developing countries make sacrifices when we ourselves are not prepared to make greater ones; and that the chances of a global agreement are maximised by Australia taking a unilateral first step, and a significant one. Both are fair points.

But the awful significance of the global nature of climate change doubtless never occurs to those who warn against Australia taking action before the rest of the world. The decisions Australia takes in relation to addressing climate change – whether to undertake unilateral action or await a global deal, how quickly or slowly it starts its transition to a low-carbon economy – will not significantly affect how seriously climate change affects our country. It is a meaningless debate, based on the assumption that Australia is master of its own destiny. In fact, Australia is at the mercy of the rest of the planet. Climate change will hit Australia faster, and sooner, than virtually anywhere else. The costs of adaptation will be greater, and be incurred sooner, here than elsewhere. We are likely already paying them now. Australia's economic future and perhaps the future viability of many currently populated areas depends heavily on the rest of the world making a determined choice to seriously address climate change, rather than on whether we decide to take action.

In such a world, our status as one of the world's leading carbon exporters is deeply ironic. When the impacts of climate change mount, and the cost to the Australian economy begins to soar, and we beg the community of nations to take strong action to curb emissions, they are unlikely to look favourably on a nation that cannot give up its own carbon addiction.

Bernard Keane

Robert Merkel

Barnaby Joyce and his denialist confrères are wrong about a great many things, but they are right about one: Australia, on its own, has an extremely limited influence on the ultimate fate of the world's climate. Therefore, as Ross Garnaut argued in his review, Australia's domestic actions in the near future matter in large part in how they contribute to achieving concerted, effective *global* action on climate change.

It should be appreciated that *any* program of action to substantially mitigate climate change will involve what sound like impossibly ambitious engineering feats. However, whatever mix of environmentally sound energy technologies and efficiency measures eventually wins out, the efforts required to switch to this mix will be a tiny fraction of our human endeavour, as crudely approximated by GDP. Compared to the massive shift in industrial production achieved during World War II, mitigating climate change *should* be a doddle, both locally and globally. The difficulty in taking action, as in the case of economic reform, to which Pearse draws apt parallels, is simple to express yet fiendishly difficult to overcome. The benefits are long-term and shared by all the world's citizens, current and future, while the costs are borne in the here and now and fall disproportionately on numerically small, but cohesive, well-organised and financially powerful groups.

But we come back to the key question: what can Australia do to achieve as much global action as possible, as quickly as possible, in the imperfect world in which we live? It is in this context that we must closely examine Pearse's proposals for the future, particularly those which concern foreign countries. We do not have time for empty gestures – while symbolism is important, it is only important in the context of convincing the entire world to sign up to the necessary action. And, like the financial crisis, sometimes we'll have to hold our nose and let thoroughly undeserving types profit along the way if it achieves a broader goal. So, for instance, while it is galling that Australians will be rewarding rent-seeking by the various multinationals that make up the carbon lobby, this will have little to no effect on the world's emissions trajectory. If buying the carbon lobby's silence will enable Australia to play a positive role in negotiating the best possible global-emissions deal, it will be cheap at the price.

So let us examine the effects of Pearse's key proposal: phasing out coal exports. As Pearse has noted, while Australia may be the world's largest coal exporter, our production represents a mere fraction of global production. And the world's coal reserves are immense. The orderly shutdown of Australia's coal industry would merely result in a lot of heavy machinery being shipped overseas to dig up coal elsewhere. Pearse is correct that it would be rather less of a disaster for the Australian economy than the coal lobby claims, but its substantive impact on the world's carbon emissions would be negligible. So we are left with the possibility that the voluntary discarding of a fairly substantial source of export income would stun the world into similar action. Frankly, I think a more likely reaction is a collective shake of the head from our customers and the continued purchase of coal, extracted using the same machinery by the same multinational companies that previously operated in Australia.

Instead, it is my view that we should concentrate on our own backyard, where black coal, and the carboniferous mud that is Victoria's and South Australia's brown coal, provide most of our electricity. V8 Commodores and Toyota Prados clog suburban streets – and, in an often neglected but very substantial source of greenhouse gas, cattle and sheep burp and fart their way across the barren, decarbonised soils of the vast interior.

In that sense, we would be far better off pricing our domestic greenhouse emissions to the hilt (through a radically beefed-up emissions trading scheme or a carbon tax) and using the revenue to subsidise the development and early deployment of clean technologies of whatever form, so that they are capable of replacing dirty coal and oil on the scale required.

Pearse's essay skirts the issue, but the hard facts are that *none* of the renewable-energy options currently available in Australia, either singly or in combination, is yet capable of permanently shutting down Australia's coal-fired power stations, let alone supplanting the fossil-fuel motor vehicle. Leaving aside cost issues for a moment, neither wind nor solar power can be relied upon to deliver energy when and where it is desired. There are any number of ideas on the drawing board, or in the early stages of development, which may overcome this problem, including various forms of energy storage and more reliable forms of renewable energy, such as hot-rock geothermal energy. I'm quite confident that, eventually, some of them will work well. But they do not exist today, however much proponents of renewable energy would like to claim that they do, and it is not at all certain that they will be available sooner, and cheaper, than carbon capture and storage (or, indeed, a domestic nuclear-power program). And they will not come to exist in our lifetimes unless government mandates (in one form or another) force their invention and commercial deployment.

It is my view that such a program of domestic emissions reduction would send at least as inspirational a moral message to the rest of the world as the largely empty gesture of phasing out coal exports. It would also achieve two other important goals. We would achieve a small but useful reduction in global greenhouse-gas emissions, buying the world a few months more to act. More importantly, forcing the wide deployment of clean-energy technologies in Australia would contribute to making the technologies available to the rest of the world, so that when China, India and the other developing nations decide to turn off the emissions from their gargantuan domestic coal sectors, the technologies that enable them to do so at an affordable cost will be more than a glint in some venture capitalist's eye.

Pearse is withering on Australia's intended use of cheap forest credits from developing countries to avoid taking any action of our own. It is indeed a major concern that cheap credits from Papua New Guinea and Indonesia will further postpone the clean-up of our domestic emissions. But we should not blind ourselves to the fact that the biosphere does not care where greenhouse-gas emissions occur and that rainforest destruction in Australia's neighbours makes a considerably greater contribution to greenhouse-gas levels than Australia's own emissions. So we should not treat the prevention of emissions from rainforests in our near neighbours as some kind of optional extra in Australia's overall strategy for mitigating climate change. Given our proximity (and in the case of Papua New Guinea, considerable influence), we should make stopping and indeed reversing that deforestation one of our highest priorities. Again, it seems to me that this would not only be morally appropriate but would also make a considerable practical difference.

All of this will be much easier to do if we continue to be supported by the ill-gotten gains of the coal industry. It may well be that, in the long run, the thermal-coal industry will die of its own accord as its export customers no longer burn coal for their electricity needs. Perhaps carbon capture and storage will be deployed widely enough to ensure a continuing market for our coal. We should indeed be prepared for the possibility that our thermal-coal industry will die, but there is no point in killing it prematurely.

The medium-term future I am sketching out for Australia may seem rather distasteful. Australia's coal exports are far more harmful than Afghani heroin or Colombian cocaine, and it would not be inappropriate for Australia to wear similar levels of international opprobrium for them. But a unilateral withdrawal from the coal trade would be as pointless as a single Afghani farmer getting out of the opium business. In the imperfect world we live in, we need to figure out how to stop the entire world from sending its future up a coal smokestack. By forcing the speedy deployment of clean technology through the application of domestic economic pressure, we can make a far bigger contribution to that urgent goal.

Robert Merkel

Brian Toohey

Guy Pearse makes a forceful case for Australia doing more to nullify the greenhouse-gas emissions from burning coal to make electricity or help smelt steel. Given the huge scale of the global emissions from coal, it is tempting to argue, as Pearse does, that Australia has a moral obligation to phase out the export of coal.

The counter-argument is not simply pragmatic. Yes, other countries may step up their exports and Kevin Rudd will never agree to an export ban. However, successful action requires all countries to co-operate in tackling global warming. Morality can play an important motivating role in achieving international agreement. It can also persuade developed countries to make a bigger initial effort in recognition of the way their past behaviour has contributed to the bulk of the problem.

But the only international remedy remotely in prospect is based on each country being responsible for reducing the emissions created within its own borders. Australia has a long way to go before it makes a reasonable contribution in this regard without taking the additional step of banning all coal exports by 2020. Apart from being well beyond the scope of any plausible international agreement, such a ban would reduce the moral pressure on other countries to cut the emissions they create by burning coal.

The first requirement for Australia is to adopt an effective policy for addressing its own emissions – something the Rudd government's corrupt version of an emissions trading scheme will never achieve. A successful scheme must generate enough revenue to fund the development and initial deployment of a wide range of abatement and low-emissions technologies, so as to establish what's cost-effective. Some of this funding should explore various options for coal, rather than persist with Rudd's folly of concentrating almost solely on carbon capture and storage, the option that is highly likely to prove a commercial failure.

Under the proposed trading scheme, none of the revenue from selling pollution permits will be spent on technologies for cutting emissions. Instead, the government is using the trading scheme as a giant churning mechanism in which all proceeds from the sale of pollution permits (around $12 billion initially) will be returned as compensation to big polluters and households. The scheme's impact on households is so small that they don't need any special compensation. Little compensation is justified for industry.

A much simpler alternative would be to start with a combination of tighter emissions standards and a low-priced levy, say $10 per tonne of carbon dioxide, gradually increasing until a full international scheme is up and running. Although it might seem paradoxical, this could provide bigger cuts to emissions than the government's new plan for a $10 price on a pollution permit in 2011, which is then estimated to jump to $25 in 2012 and escalate thereafter. The reason is that the levy could be used to fund the deployment of low emissions technology, unlike the revenue from pollution permits, which Kevin Rudd proposes to waste on unjustified compensation – a decision that only adds to the difficulties of achieving the cuts imposed by government regulation under the cap and trade scheme.

There are three main ways the Australian coal industry might survive. One would be to extract far more energy from coal, so that much less CO_2 is produced. For example, it is technically feasible to use coal in a direct carbon fuel cell, which relies on an electro-chemical process to generate electricity. Because the potential efficiency of these cells is over 90 per cent, they produce only a small stream of pure CO_2 involving no separation or capture costs.

Another possibility is to convert CO_2 into something of value. Options include reducing CO_2 to formic acid for use in fuel cells or as a feedstock for various chemicals. Other suggestions entail converting CO_2 into propane or a hard carbonate building material. Power-station flue gases could be diverted into bio-reactors to promote the growth of algae for making biodiesel. Another promising option is to make cement by bubbling flue gases through sea water. All are interesting; all have yet to reach the stage where their financial worth can be established.

But the industry and government have picked carbon capture and storage. Pearse sets out some of the reasons why it will struggle to prove financially viable. CCS uses about 30 per cent of a power plant's energy output to separate CO_2 from other flue gases, capture it, compress it and transport it via specially constructed pipelines for permanent storage after it is injected into suitable geological reservoirs, which are often only available in uneconomic locations. Attempts to reduce the costs of separating the CO2 by first gasifying coal, or burning it in oxygen, incur other financial penalties.

CCS is generally estimated to double the cost of generating electricity from coal. This poses a huge challenge for the coal industry when alternative fuel sources, such as geothermal power, have zero emissions and are projected to produce base-load electricity within a few years for less than low-emissions coal-fired stations. The costs of wind, wave and solar power are also falling. An indication of the scale of the funding problem for CCS can be seen from the proposed ZeroGen 80-megawatt demonstration plant in Queensland, which is estimated to cost $1.7 billion. This contrasts with the $300 million the West Australian wave-power company Carnegie proposes spending on a 50-megawatt demonstration plant to produce zero-emissions base-load electricity and desalinated water.

As Pearse notes, biochar (made from heating organic material in the absence of oxygen) is a potential substitute for coal in steel smelting. It also has a good prospect of sequestering carbon commercially and producing renewable energy, with added value if used to enhance soil quality.

If, against all the odds, CCS works on a massive scale, that's good. If not, there are many alternative pathways to developing clean sources of energy. Provided serious funding is available, something will almost certainly succeed in delivering big cuts to emissions without the need to ban coal exports. Most likely, they will simply fade away.

Brian Toohey

John Hewson

Kevin is right! Even if he doesn't actually believe it, climate change is the moral issue of our generation, not to mention the economic, social and political issue. It is bigger, and much more urgent, than yet conceded in the "debate."

Time is of the essence, and it is fast running out. The appropriate policy responses must be front-end loaded. It will be impossible to play catch-up against essential 2050 targets for emissions reductions.

Unfortunately, we are lost in a contest in the 24-hour media cycle, where the key players focus solely on scoring short-term political points against each other, where the most vocal and best-funded vested interests easily hold sway, and where the media are more interested in colour, movement and political cleverness than substance.

In none of this is there much evidence that our political and business leaders really understand – and certainly they do not accept – the nature and magnitude of the challenge. It is not just another development, or policy or market failure, that can be "fixed" by a marginal adjustment in government tax or spending policies.

The challenge is to make the transition to a new society, not just a new economy, from the carbon-intensive, oil- and fossil-fuel based society, which has proved unsustainable, to a low-carbon society. As such, we seek a new vision, a new culture, a new lifestyle – which, in turn, calls for a holistic rethink by governments, businesses and individuals.

To economists, the answer is relatively straightforward: put a market price on carbon, make the polluters pay, in the context of meaningful targets, and all the rest will follow. Investors will shift their investments to alternative energy and technologies, businesses will understand and reduce their carbon footprint, consumers will change their consumption and behaviour. And we'll all wake up one day in a low-carbon world.

But our politicians, driven by the big polluters and others who would claim to be worse off, and wanting to be seen to be doing something, step in to "fix it." Game on!

Enter Guy Pearse with the courage to address some of the "grubbiness" of this process, but offering a realistic assessment of where we are, and of how we need to, and can, go forward from the mire of today. His contributions to the necessary debate are most significant. I sincerely hope that Guy is read widely, but I fear that against the vested interests he has evidenced, and in the context of the political games being played, he too risks being left high and dry.

Let me make a couple of specific points. First, even if we accept – which I don't – that clean coal can be a silver-bullet response to climate change, how is it that the focus is on carbon capture and storage to the exclusion of alternatives? All the evidence that I have seen suggests that CCS is unlikely ever to be commercially viable, costing as much as $100 per tonne to liquefy, transport and store. Yet the government is committing some $100 million a year to the institute to "prove it up," in the face of other alternatives such as algae, which could be proved up at a one-off fraction of the annual cost.

Secondly, to make one of Guy's points more bluntly, for a carbon price to work economically, as established by (say) a genuine emissions trading scheme, compensation must be kept to a minimum. It is the price that drives the change in behaviour; otherwise you should rely on mandating: ban incandescent light bulbs, mandate bio-fuels, ban coal-fired power plants, and so on. In reality, you will probably need both approaches.

Finally, Guy is right to suggest that Australia can lead the world on the climate-change challenge, not just claim to do so, as both Howard and Rudd have done. As a middle-ranking power, but a globally significant polluter per capita, we can genuinely punch above our weight by setting what could easily become a global benchmark in response.

What should have already been done? We should have admitted that our 2050 target for emissions reductions should be more like 90 per cent, with the interim, front-end loaded target, for 2020, of some 40 per cent to be achieved by a "pure" ETS with an independent, Reserve Bank-style "auctioneer" and allocator of compensation.

This would need to be backed up with a host of government policies to encourage investment in the development of alternative technologies, a change of government procurement policies, and a clear statement of what should become a national vision of a low-carbon economy, which promises new industries and stronger and sustainable growth and employment.

As tough as it will be to extricate ourselves from the most significant economic and financial crisis since the Great Depression, this is *not* a choice. Indeed, a sustainable recovery will be in a low-debt, low-carbon economy.

John Hewson

Correspondence

David Karoly

Quarry Vision presents an alarming picture of the role played by lobby groups for the coal and mining industries in Australia. At the same time, scientific under-standing of climate change and its impacts is increasing rapidly, reinforcing the urgent need to reduce greenhouse-gas emissions. The recent International Scientific Congress, *Climate Change: Global Risks, Challenges & Decisions*, in Copenhagen in March 2009, attended by more than 2500 delegates from almost eighty countries, agreed on a number of key messages:

> Recent observations show that societies are highly vulnerable to even modest levels of climate change, with poor nations and communities particularly at risk. Temperature rises above 2 degrees Celsius will be very difficult for contemporary societies to cope with, and will increase the level of climate disruption through the rest of the century.
>
> Rapid, sustained, and effective mitigation based on coordinated global and regional action is required to avoid 'dangerous climate change' regardless of how it is defined. Weaker targets for 2020 increase the risk of crossing tipping points and make the task of meeting 2050 targets more difficult. Delay in initiating effective mitigation actions increases significantly the long-term social and economic costs of both adaptation and mitigation.

On 19 March 2009, the Parliament of Australia's Joint Standing Committee on Treaties tabled its report on *Review of the Kyoto Protocol to the United Nations Framework Convention on Climate Change*. That review concluded "it is in Australia's interests to secure global agreement to deliver deep cuts in emissions so as to stabilise concentrations of greenhouse gases in the atmosphere at 450 parts per million or lower by 2050."

So, what is needed to stabilise greenhouse-gas concentrations at a level that would avoid temperature rises above 2 degrees Celsius? The IPCC's *Fourth Assessment Report*, released in 2007, considered various scenarios, based on published scientific studies. The lowest scenario, for stabilisation at 445–490ppm CO2-e and best-estimate global average temperature increases of 2.0 degrees to 2.4 degrees Celsius, requires global CO2 emissions to peak in 2000–2015, and global CO2 emissions to be reduced by 50 per cent to 85 per cent in 2050 relative to 2000. Note that this scenario gives a more than 50 per cent likelihood of global average temperature increases exceeding 2 degrees Celsius, the threshold for dangerous climate change used by the EU. It also gives a 5 per cent likelihood of global average temperature increases greater than 4.3 degrees Celsius.

These very large reductions are needed because the concentration of long-lived greenhouse gases in the atmosphere in 2005 was 455ppm CO2-e, already exceeding the 450ppm long-term stabilisation level. The concentration in 2008 was above 460ppm CO2-e. Hence, greenhouse gases need to be removed from the atmosphere to achieve this stabilisation level, rather than further increased.

To achieve long-term stabilisation at around 450ppm CO2-e, the IPCC concluded that developed countries would need to reduce their emissions by 25 to 40 per cent in 2020 relative to 1990 levels, and by 80 to 95 per cent in 2050. Using a "converge and contract" approach, which leads in time to approximately equal per-capita global emissions, 50 to 85 per cent reductions in global CO2 emissions in 2050 corresponds to *Australian emission reductions of 90 to 97 per cent in 2050.*

Urgent action to reduce greenhouse-gas emissions is essential. Any delay increases significantly the long-term social and economic costs of both adaptation and mitigation. Quarry vision is preventing necessary action. Current coal-fired power stations have no future in Australia. They must be either closed and replaced by alternative energy sources, or converted to effective carbon capture and storage solutions within the next decade. The British government, recognising the need for these changes, has just announced that no new coal-fired power stations will be built in Britain unless they capture and bury at least 25 per cent of greenhouse gases immediately and 100 per cent by 2025.

Addressing climate change needs national and international leadership. Unfortunately, quarry vision has been leading us in exactly the wrong direction.

David Karoly

Guy Pearse

The notion that Australia is blinded by a "quarry vision" that renders its political leaders incapable of deeply cutting greenhouse pollution at home is apparently uncontroversial. Barring a few issues raised in correspondence here – mostly relating to coal exports – there's been no serious attempt to challenge what was argued in *Quarry Vision*. Maybe that's because it is stating the obvious to stress how habitually Australia inflates the dollars and jobs created by its mining, metals and resources sectors. As for the beneficiaries of quarry vision, our worst polluting industries and their political accomplices, well, they know better than to respond.

The only official reply to *Quarry Vision* came in response to my claim that the Rudd government planned to let Australia outsource almost all of its greenhouse obligations. Rather than cutting emissions here (as Rudd had promised), we'd allow polluters to, among other things, pay our near neighbours not to log their forests, and then take credit for the carbon stored. In response to comments I made about this on Radio National Breakfast in March, neither Penny Wong nor Ross Garnaut even tried to deny this agenda. On the contrary, they tried to make a virtue of it, asking what was wrong with us paying others to store our emissions in their forests if that is cheaper than reducing the greenhouse pollution from Australian smokestacks and tailpipes?

This devil-may-care approach to who makes emission cuts and where they actually occur made Wong's comparison between tackling climate change and getting fit especially breathtaking. "We have been talking about responding to climate change for years now," she said. "You don't get fit by saying you want to get fit. You get fit by having a plan to get there. Australia needs a plan to reduce its emissions. That's what we've put forward." Only it wasn't! Under the plan being promoted by Wong, Australia could effectively pay someone else to get fit on its behalf, and we could take the credit. Like one of those "too good to be true" infomercials, Australia could do its bit on climate change without doing any heavy lifting. Forget this "no pain, no gain" palaver. We needn't shed a single kilo, let alone a tonne of carbon.

The debate drifts languidly on. Our biggest contribution to climate change – our coal exports – is never mentioned, and it is as if the outsourcing agenda was never exposed, let alone confirmed. Two fossilised parties thereby get away without explaining just how crucial their outsourcing plans are to the seemingly incompatible objectives of meeting even bigger emissions reduction targets and giving even bigger handouts to polluters. The race to the bottom worsened in May as the government realised the only hope of Senate passage for its emissions trading legislation was further capitulation to polluters, in order to win Liberal Party support. The starting date was pushed beyond the next election, the compensation to polluters was increased, and the permit price was capped at $10 for the first year. The biggest polluters – aluminium smelters for example – would now pay for only 1 in every 20 tonnes of their greenhouse pollution. Needless to say, the government said it was "strengthening" the scheme.

Farcically, sections of the green movement welcomed the government's watering down of the scheme. WWF, the Climate Institute and the Australian Conservation Foundation got behind the legislation and declared it "time to move on." They said that it was a "hard call," but in the end the government's decision to "officially consider" a 25 per cent target was the clincher. They might have cautiously welcomed official consideration of a heavily conditional 25 per cent target without actually backing the legislation, but no. Their inexplicable behaviour perpetuated the fantasy that the current approach can "maximise sustainable jobs growth in the emerging global low-carbon economic recovery" even if all of Australia's emission cuts are made offshore. By implicitly endorsing Kevin Rudd's outsourcing agenda, they now help to fuel the prospect that, in a few years, Australia will claim to be "on track" to meet ambitious targets even though no cuts have been made to greenhouse pollution at home. Instead, the pollution will be hidden in trees – just as it was when John Howard used avoided deforestation in Queensland to claim we were on track to meet our Kyoto target even as actual greenhouse pollution spiralled. The old saying seems apt: as long as you keep doing what you've always done, you'll keep getting what you've always got. Such is life in Australia's climate-policy debate: the same people doing the same thing with familiar results.

Against the backdrop of that inertia, I welcome the correspondence that various prominent Australians have offered. I'm tempted to imagine an Australia in which some of them played different roles: imagine a Liberal prime minister arguing for a 40 per cent reduction by 2020, bringing in an emissions trading scheme without polluter handouts, and mandating a ban on coal-fired power stations. Imagine a chief scientist arguing that coal-fired power stations need to be shut down or cleaned up within a decade. Imagine Bernard Keane writing climate-change editorials at the *Australian*.

Across the diverse group of correspondents it was heartening to see a consensus and deep concern surrounding the grip that quarry vision has on our political establishment. Patrice Newell laments the "gravitational pull of coal's easy money" and its contaminating influence. We learn that no coal-mining application has ever been knocked back in New South Wales – and why would it with the federal government funding infrastructure to double coal exports? It is an intergovernmental see-saw where another coal-friendly response seems the only option, and ignorance is bliss (ask Greg Combet if he's heard of James Hansen).

Perhaps unsurprisingly, most of the correspondence focuses on my support for a phase-down of Australia's coal industry by 2020 in the event that carbon capture and storage cannot prevent its greenhouse-gas emissions. The main misgivings are predictable: that Australia's withdrawal from the coal trade will have little impact on global emissions; that others will take our place in the coal trade; that there is no substitute for coking coal to make steel; and that coal will die a natural death if CCS fails. Collectively, these arguments are symptomatic of quarry vision and the notion that dealing with coal now is just too hard – much easier to focus on other things and hope for the best.

Curiously, the argument that cutting coal exports makes no difference to global emissions is mounted here by someone advocating domestic actions that would also make no difference to global emissions. Robert Merkel says we should "concentrate on our own backyard" rather than on coal exports. He calls the negligible impact Australia might have, even if it cut its domestic emissions to zero, "a small but useful reduction in global greenhouse-gas emissions," yet he calls eliminating comparable emissions exported via our coal a "symbolic," "empty gesture." It's puzzling that an advocate of domestic action should co-opt the "carbon leakage" argument most often used by sceptics and polluters alike against domestic emission cuts by Australia: that it would be a symbolic and empty gesture because of its negligible impact on global emissions.

Just as the carbon lobby has argued that domestic action would merely move Australian production offshore, Merkel contends that a phasing out of coal in Australia would simply shift coal-digging machinery offshore. He skates past the significant impact that an Australian "sunset on coal" would have on global confidence in the coal trade on the part of investors and consumers. I'm genuinely surprised he has no qualms about resorting to the drug dealer's defence: someone else will supply it if we don't. If Australian coal is in fact "more harmful than Afghani heroin and Colombian cocaine," as Merkel says, it makes little sense to argue that the removal of Australian coal is no more significant than the removal of one Afghani heroin grower. The similarity between these drug trades and Australian coal is perhaps more telling insofar as all of these harmful industries depend on complicit or impotent governments to survive and thrive.

Sooner rather than later we must recognise that the decisions we make about our coal exports determine whether our domestic action makes any real difference. Growth in the emissions caused by Australia's projected coal exports would erase all the emissions we might save domestically over the next two decades. Ultimately, we cannot have a credible domestic response while we ignore our greatest contribution to the problem. Why not do both and maximise the impact we make on the global equation?

Patrice Newell argues that campaigners must differentiate and focus on thermal coal rather than metallurgical coal on the grounds that "we still need steel." Of course we still need electricity too, but while Newell is justifiably confident that we can deliver that without coal burning, she is not ready to imagine a steel industry without coal – not even by 2020, it seems. It's "reckless and immoral to keep bankrolling thermal coal," but bankrolling coal-based steel production is somehow okay. This double standard ignores various realities: that we produced steel without coal for thousands of years; that the steel industry itself has invested heavily in confirming (with CSIRO's help) that biochar can largely replace coking coal in steel production. Moreover, it ignores the reality that no commodity is sacred. Stripping the global economy of 90 per cent of its carbon emissions over the next few decades will inevitably mean switching away from those commodities for which no commercially viable clean solution can be found, and that may include steel. With coking coal accounting for around half of the emissions we export, the sooner we get our heads around that, the better. As Newell says of coal-fired electricity, let's start.

Brian Toohey takes refuge in the idea that we are not responsible for emissions that occur beyond our borders. Presumably Saudi Arabia should not care less about the emissions from its oil, either. Toohey even suggests that if Australia phased out its coal exports, it would reduce the moral pressure on other countries to cut the emissions generated by coal use. The corollary is that the best way to put pressure on other countries is to export more coal to them – an absurd notion. If CCS fails to deliver on a meaningful scale in time (which is odds-on), Robert Merkel suspects the coal industry "dies of its own accord."

For his part, Toohey thinks coal exports "will simply fade away." A decade of investigating Australia's greenhouse mafia – particularly its coal industry – suggests to me this is not exactly their style. It is also completely at odds with the breakneck expansion of coal production now occurring in this country. The only thing more foolish than banking on CCS to deliver on scale on time is banking on the coal industry shutting up shop if it doesn't. If CCS works, Merkel imagines Australia can make even more money selling China and India the technology along with the coal. However, it will be a very long wait for those cheques, what with Treasury saying that they don't expect commercial deployment of CCS in Australia (let alone elsewhere) until 2033. If the money ever does arrive, David Karoly's comments here suggest it will be decades too late. What of the damage done in the meantime?

When it comes to making deep cuts in the greenhouse pollution that Australia fuels here and abroad, quarry vision is the biggest obstacle. We prevaricate and procrastinate only to protect a quarry we wrongly regard as sacrosanct – especially its coal. Only when we appreciate that the quarry is not the economic backbone we imagine it is will we make decisions from a position of clarity and strength rather than fear and weakness. When this finally happens, "our" coal industry (it's overwhelmingly foreign-owned) will naturally try to take the same approach as did the producers of asbestos, tobacco and other harmful products. While they legally can, they will seek to operate in and supply countries in more desperate economic circumstances. That is much more their style than dying a natural death and fading away. But knowing that is their likely agenda doesn't make it any more right for us to prolong their operations here. The unanswered question for those reluctant to tackle coal is the same one I posed in *Quarry Vision* – if not now, when: 2015, 2020, 2030 ...?

Guy Pearse

Annabel Crabb is the *Sydney Morning Herald*'s political sketchwriter and appears regularly on ABC TV's *Insiders*. She is the author of *Losing It: The Inside Story of the Labor Party in Opposition* (2005).

John Hewson is a former leader of the Liberal Party. He currently runs his own investment banking business and writes an opinion column for the *Australian Financial Review*.

David Karoly is professor of meteorology at the University of Melbourne and a lead author of the IPCC's *Fourth Assessment Report* (2007).

Bernard Keane is *Crikey*'s political correspondent in Canberra.

Robert Merkel is a postdoctoral research fellow in software engineering at Swinburne University of Technology. He has a blog called *The View from Benambra*.

Patrice Newell was a newsreader and broadcaster on SBS and Channel Nine. She is the author of several books on sustainable farming and a co-founder of the Climate Change Coalition.

Guy Pearse is a former member of the Liberal Party and was a speechwriter for former environment minister Robert Hill. He has also been an industry lobbyist, consultant and spin doctor. In 2007 he exposed the politics behind Australia's response to climate change on *Four Corners* and in his book *High & Dry*.

Brian Toohey is a columnist and feature writer for the *Australian Financial Review*, and a former editor of the *National Times*.

Subscribe to
QUARTERLY ESSAY

Subscriptions Receive a discount and never miss an issue. Mailed direct to your door.

☐ **1 year subscription** (4 issues): $49 a year within Australia incl. GST. Outside Australia $79.

☐ **2 year subscription** (8 issues): $95 a year within Australia incl. GST. Outside Australia $155.

* All prices include postage and handling.

Back Issues (Prices include postage and handling.)

☐ **QE 1** ($10.95) Robert Manne *In Denial*

☐ **QE 2** ($10.95) John Birmingham *Appeasing Jakarta*

☐ **QE 4** ($10.95) Don Watson *Rabbit Syndrome*

☐ **QE 5** ($12.95) Mungo MacCallum *Girt by Sea*

☐ **QE 6** ($12.95) John Button *Beyond Belief*

☐ **QE 7** ($12.95) John Martinkus *Paradise Betrayed*

☐ **QE 8** ($12.95) Amanda Lohrey *Groundswell*

☐ **QE 10** ($13.95) Gideon Haigh *Bad Company*

☐ **QE 11** ($13.95) Germaine Greer *Whitefella Jump Up*

☐ **QE 12** ($13.95) David Malouf *Made in England*

☐ **QE 13** ($13.95) Robert Manne with David Corlett
  Sending Them Home

☐ **QE 14** ($14.95) Paul McGeough *Mission Impossible*

☐ **QE 15** ($14.95) Margaret Simons *Latham's World*

☐ **QE 16** ($14.95) Raimond Gaita *Breach of Trust*

☐ **QE 17** ($14.95) John Hirst *"Kangaroo Court"*

☐ **QE 18** ($14.95) Gail Bell *The Worried Well*

☐ **QE 19** ($15.95) Judith Brett *Relaxed & Comfortable*

☐ **QE 20** ($15.95) John Birmingham *A Time for War*

☐ **QE 21** ($15.95) Clive Hamilton *What's Left?*

☐ **QE 22** ($15.95) Amanda Lohrey *Voting for Jesus*

☐ **QE 23** ($15.95) Inga Clendinnen *The History Question*

☐ **QE 24** ($15.95) Robyn Davidson *No Fixed Address*

☐ **QE 25** ($15.95) Peter Hartcher *Bipolar Nation*

☐ **QE 26** ($15.95) David Marr *His Master's Voice*

☐ **QE 27** ($15.95) Ian Lowe *Reaction Time*

☐ **QE 28** ($15.95) Judith Brett *Exit Right*

☐ **QE 29** ($16.95) Anne Manne *Love & Money*

☐ **QE30** ($16.95) Paul Toohey *Last Drinks*

☐ **QE31** ($16.95) Tim Flannery *Now or Never*

☐ **QE32** ($16.95) Kate Jennings *American Revolution*

☐ **QE33** ($16.95) Guy Pearse *Quarry Vision*

Payment Details I enclose a cheque/money order made out to Schwartz Media Pty Ltd.
Please debit my credit card (Mastercard, Visa or Bankcard accepted).

Card No. ☐☐☐☐ ☐☐☐☐ ☐☐☐☐ ☐☐☐☐

Expiry date   /   **Amount $**

Cardholder's name   **Signature**

Name

Address

Email

Post or Fax this form to: Quarterly Essay, Reply Paid 79448, Melbourne, VIC 3000
Freecall: 1800 077 514 / Fax: 61 3 9654 2290 / Email: subscribe@blackincbooks.com

Subscribe online at **www.quarterlyessay.com**